Working Words in Spelling

REVISED EDITION

G. Willard Woodruff and George N. Moore
with Robert G. Forest, Richard A. Talbot, Ann R. Talbot

HEATH
D.C. Heath and Company
Lexington, Massachusetts / Toronto, Ontario

CONTENTS

Acknowledgments follow on page 176.

Published simultaneously in Canada

Printed in the United States of America

International Standard Book Number: 0-669-31390-4

2 3 4 5 6 7 8 9 10-BA-99 98 97 96 95 94

Become a **S-H-A-R-P** Speller

See the word.

- Look at the word.
- Think about the letters that spell the word.

Hear the word.

- Say the word.
- Listen to the consonant and vowel sounds.

Adopt the word.

- Close your eyes.
- See the word in your mind's eye.
- Think how it looks and sounds.

Record the word.

- Cover the word.
- Write the word.

Proofread the word.

- Correct the word.
- Touch each letter.
- Think about the word again.

1

A. Pretest and Proofreading

B. Spelling Words and Phrases

1.	**fade**	will <u>fade</u> in the light
2.	**wade**	to wade into the water
3.	**cape**	wool cape
4.	**races**	relay races
5.	**dare**	if you dare
6.	**he's**	if he's ready
7.	**she's**	if she's going
8.	**being**	being very unkind
9.	**meet**	will meet at the game
10.	**seemed**	seemed to know
11.	**mile**	one mile away
12.	**pile**	pile of sand
13.	**dive**	a shallow dive
14.	**size**	a different size
15.	**alike**	look alike
16.	**hire**	will hire the student

Other Word Forms

faded, fading
wades, waded, wading
capes
race, raced, racing
dares, dared, daring
be, been, am, is
met, meeting
seem, seems, seeming
miles
piles, piled, piling
dives, dived, dove, diving, diver
sizes
alikeness
hired, hiring

C. Visual Warm-up Write each word in its correct shape.

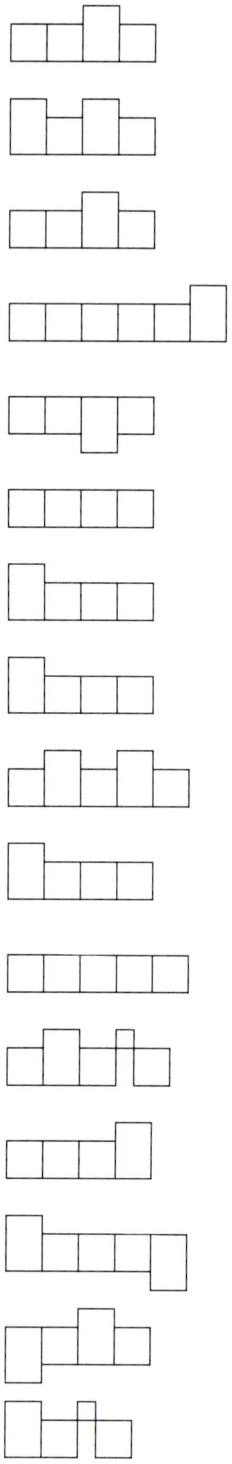

a.
b.
c.
d.
e.
f.
g.
h.
i.
j.
k.
l.
m.
n.
o.
p.

D. All in a Row Write the sixteen spelling words in alphabetical order. Then join the boxed letters and write four hidden words.

1. ___ ___ ___ ☐ ___
2. ___ ___ ___ ☐ ___
3. ___ ___ ___ ☐
4. ___ ___ ___ ☐
5. Hidden Word: ________________

6. ☐ ___ ___ ___
7. ___ ___ ___ ☐
8. ___ ☐ ___
9. ___ ___ ☐ ___
10. Hidden Word: ________________

11. ___ ___ ___ ☐
12. ___ ☐ ___ ___
13. ___ ___ ___ ☐
14. ___ ___ ___ ___ ☐
15. Hidden Word: ________________

16. ☐ ___ ___ ___ ___ ___
17. ___ ☐ ___ ___
18. ___ ___ ___ ☐
19. ___ ___ ☐ ___
20. Hidden Word: ________________

E. What Am I? Solve each word mystery with a spelling word.

1. I'm a walk in the water. ___ ___ ___ ___
2. I'm 5,280 feet. ___ ___ ___ ___
3. I'm a sleeveless coat. ___ ___ ___ ___
4. I'm a favorite of fast runners. ___ ___ ___ ___ ___
5. I'm a leap into water. ___ ___ ___ ___
6. I'm a heap of things. ___ ___ ___ ___
7. I'm a 15 shirt or a 12 dress. ___ ___ ___ ___
8. I'm a challenge. ___ ___ ___ ___

Spelling Words

fade wade cape races dare he's she's
being meet seemed mile pile dive size
alike hire

F. Crossword Puzzle Solve the puzzle by using words from the spelling list. Write each word. Check your answers in the **Spelling Dictionary**.

Across

2. to dim
5. acting in a certain way
6. appeared
8. he is (contraction)

Down

1. to pay for work
3. similar
4. she is (contraction)
7. to come together

G. Finding Words The words in the spelling list appear in the beginning (A-H), middle (I-Q), or end (R-Z) of the **Spelling Dictionary**. Write each word.

Beginning A-H

1. ____________
2. ____________
3. ____________
4. ____________
5. ____________
6. ____________
7. ____________
8. ____________

Middle I-Q

9. ____________
10. ____________
11. ____________

End R-Z

12. ____________
13. ____________
14. ____________
15. ____________
16. ____________

H. Using Other Word Forms Add an ending to each word to write an Other Word Form.

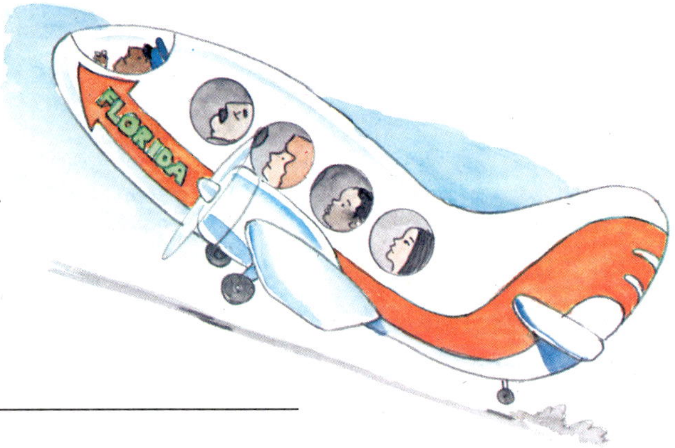

1. fade + ing = __ __ __ __ __ __
2. race + ing = __ __ __ __ __ __
3. dare + ing = __ __ __ __ __ __
4. pile + ing = __ __ __ __ __ __
5. hire + ing = __ __ __ __ __ __
6. What letter keeps disappearing? ____________

I. Challenge Words Write the Challenge Word that completes each question.

agent	airline	aware	degrees	gazing

1. Did you ever fly on that ____________ ?
2. How many ____________ did the temperature drop?
3. Do you have an insurance ____________ ?
4. Who is ____________ at the picture?
5. Are you ____________ of the problem?

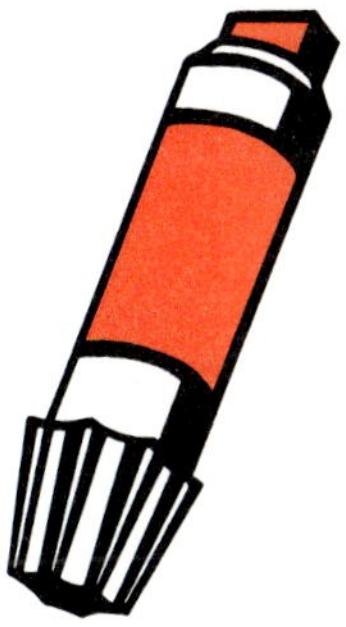

J. Spelling and Writing Write each set of words in a sentence. You may use Other Word Forms. Proofread your work.

Example: he's – meet—*He's going to meet us at the park.*

1. he's – pile
2. she's – cape
3. being – dive
4. meet – races
5. seemed – fade
6. dare – wade
7. hire – mile
8. alike – size
9. agent – airline
10. aware – gazing
11. degrees – seems

2

A. Pretest and Proofreading

B. Spelling Words and Phrases

1.	woke	woke up early
2.	holes	holes in my socks
3.	won't	won't try again
4.	tore	tore the shirt
5.	wore	wore old clothes
6.	ax	sharpened the ax
7.	rack	storage rack
8.	backward	backward somersault
9.	draft	a cold draft
10.	can't	can't argue about it
11.	camel	camel in the desert
12.	madly	was running madly
13.	began	began all over
14.	mapping	mapping the city
15.	crossing	crossing the street
16.	across	across and down

Other Word Forms

wake, waking, wakes
hole
torn, tear, tears, tearing
wear, wears, wearing, worn
axes
racks
backwards
drafts
camels
mad, madder, maddest
begin, begins, beginning
map, maps, mapped
cross, crosses, crossed

C. Visual Warm-up

Write each word in its correct shape.

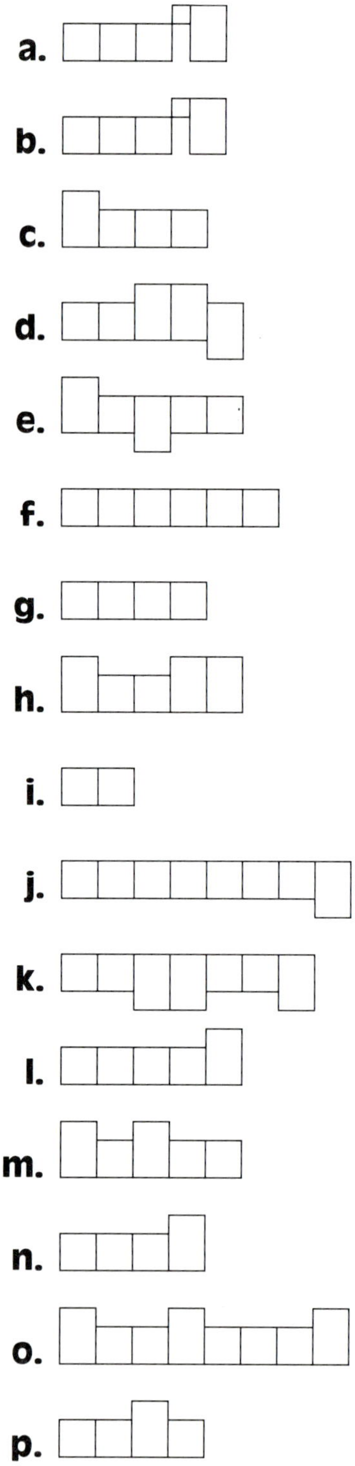

D. Missing Vowels Find the missing vowels and write the spelling words.

1. dr ___ ft ____________
2. c ___ m ___ l ____________
3. m ___ pp ___ ng ____________
4. w ___ r ___ ____________
5. b ___ g ___ n ____________
6. w ___ k ___ ____________
7. cr ___ ss ___ ng ____________
8. b ___ ckw ___ rd ____________
9. h ___ l ___ s ____________
10. c ___ n't ____________
11. w ___ n't ____________
12. ___ cr ___ ss ____________
13. t ___ r ___ ____________
14. m ___ dl ___ ____________
15. ___ x ____________
16. r ___ ck ____________

E. Hide and Seek The spelling words can be found in the word puzzle. The words appear across and down. Circle and write the words.

b	e	g	a	n	t	c	w	o
a	c	e	x	s	s	r	o	m
c	a	n	t	o	t	o	r	e
k	m	a	d	l	y	s	e	n
w	e	a	c	r	o	s	s	t
a	l	m	a	p	p	i	n	g
r	a	c	k	w	o	n	t	e
d	r	a	f	t	d	g	o	o
h	o	l	e	s	w	o	k	e

Across

1. ____________
2. ____________
3. ____________
4. ____________
5. ____________
6. ____________
7. ____________
8. ____________
9. ____________
10. ____________
11. ____________

Down

12. ____________
13. ____________
14. ____________
15. ____________
16. ____________

Spelling Words

woke	holes	won't	tore	wore	ax
rack	backward	draft	can't	camel	madly
began	mapping	crossing	across		

F. Word Riddles Write the spelling word that answers each riddle.

1. Making a plan of your neighborhood ______
2. What the nail did to your pants ______
3. What clothes hang on ______
4. An animal that is handy in the desert ______
5. What you dug in the ground ______
6. The opposite of *forward* ______
7. The first thing you did this morning ______
8. What you used to cut a tree ______
9. Where you and a chicken went on the road ______
10. What you did when you started ______
11. How you worked when in a rush ______
12. The opposite of *will* ______
13. The opposite of *can* ______
14. A cool place you try to avoid ______
15. What you should be doing to all your *t*'s ______
16. What you did with your new sweater ______

G. Using Other Word Forms Write the Other Word Form that completes each series.

Base Words: map(ed) wake(ing) tear(ing) begin(ing) wear(ing)

1. wakes, woke, ______________
2. tears, tore, ______________
3. wears, wore, ______________
4. begins, began, ______________
5. maps, ______________ , mapping

H. Challenge Words Write the Challenge Word that fits each group of words.

slope	**tomorrow**	**actor**	**fought**	**watermelon**

1. pilot, teacher, ______________
2. lemon, orange, ______________
3. yesterday, today, ______________
4. hill, incline, ______________
5. argued, debated, ______________

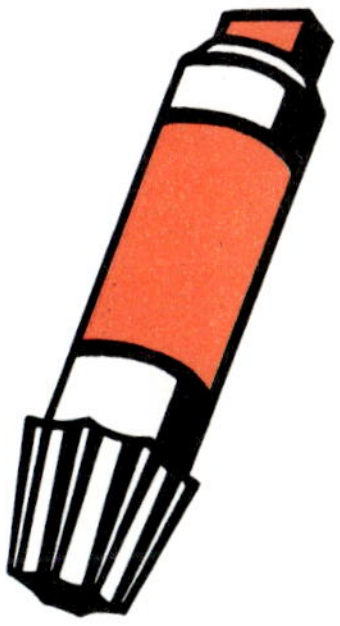

I. Spelling and Writing Read the story idea. Use the Spelling Words, Other Word Forms, and Challenge Words to help you think of an answer to each question. Proofread your work.

Story idea:
The house they entered was drafty, dark, and haunted.

1. Where was the house located?

   Example: *The house was located on the slope of a steep hill.*
2. How did the house look from the outside?
3. Who entered the house?
4. Why did they go inside?
5. What did they see inside the house?
6. How did they know the house was haunted?

3

A. Pretest and Proofreading

B. Spelling Words and Phrases

1.	**sum**	a sum of money
2.	**plum**	a ripe plum
3.	**lump**	lump of clay
4.	**lung**	a lung illness
5.	**hunter**	hunter in the woods
6.	**begun**	had begun adding
7.	**lace**	lace tablecloth
8.	**fate**	the fate of wild animals
9.	**cases**	cases of books
10.	**saves**	saves stamps
11.	**didn't**	didn't even know
12.	**it's**	if it's possible
13.	**itself**	the job itself
14.	**swift**	swift motion
15.	**begin**	will begin to wonder
16.	**enter**	will enter the race

Other Word Forms

sums, summed, summary
plums
lumpy, lumps
lungs
hunt, hunts
began, begins, beginning
lace, laces, lacing, laced, lacy
fates
case
save, saved, saving
swiftest, swiftly
enters, entrance

C. Visual Warm-up

Write each word in its correct shape.

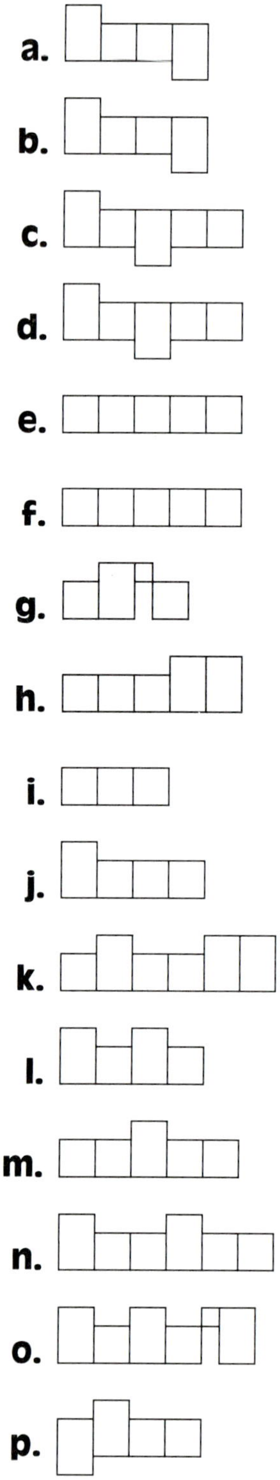

D. Scrambled Words Unscramble the scrambled word to find the spelling word that completes the sentence. Write the word.

1. The race is about to ________________ (binge).
2. He has a small ________________ (mpul) on his head.
3. Careful driving ________________ (svase) lives.
4. A prune is a dried ________________ (umpl).
5. ________________ (t'is) time for the mail carrier to come.
6. The banker has a large ________________ (ums) of money.
7. We have not ________________ (unbeg) to fight.
8. Put the blankets in the cardboard ________________ (asecs).
9. ________________ (feat) can play foolish games with a person.
10. Kindergarten children can ________________ (cale) their own shoes.
11. You must ________________ (renet) from the side door.
12. The gill of a fish is similar to a ________________ (ungl).
13. The door appeared to open by ________________ (elfist).
14. The batter is a ________________ (ftisw) runner.
15. The dogs ________________ (n'tidd) bark last night.
16. The ________________ (herunt) circled the woods.

E. Finding Words The words in the spelling list appear in the beginning (A-H), middle (I-Q), or end (R-Z) of the **Spelling Dictionary**. Write each word.

Beginning A-H	Middle I-Q	End R-Z
1. ________	8. ________	14. ________
2. ________	9. ________	15. ________
3. ________	10. ________	16. ________
4. ________	11. ________	
5. ________	12. ________	
6. ________	13. ________	
7. ________		

Spelling Words

sum	plum	lump	lung	hunter	begun
lace	fate	cases	saves	didn't	it's
itself	swift	begin	enter		

F. Lines that Rhyme Write a set of lines that rhyme. The first line in each set is done for you. Use a spelling word or an Other Word Form (p. 12) in the second line.

1. He had to jump

   Over the lump.

2. She pounded the drum

   ____

3. If he is late

   ____

4. The boat began to drift

   ____

5. The song was sung

   ____

6. If she plans to win

   ____

7. All kinds of faces

   ____

8. We started to hum

   ____

9. It was a strange case

   ____

10. We stood in the center

    ____

11. They all began to run

    ____

12. There was a space on the shelf

    ____

13. A joke or a stunt

    ____

14. They entered the cave

    ____

15. What two spelling words had no rhyming words?

    ____

    ____

G. Using Other Word Forms Write the Other Word Form that fits each group of words.

Base Words: lump(y) swift(ly) lace(ing) enter(ance) save(ing)

1. doorway, gate, hall, ____________________
2. tying, knotting, securing, ____________________
3. keeping, protecting, rescuing, ____________________
4. fast, quickly, rapidly, ____________________
5. not smooth, bumpy, chunky, ____________________

H. Challenge Words Write the Challenge Word that completes each phrase.

riddle	**weather**	**dizzy**	**plumber**	**younger**

1. either older or ____________________
2. either a puzzle or a ____________________
3. either a carpenter or a ____________________
4. either climate or ____________________
5. either clear-headed or ____________________

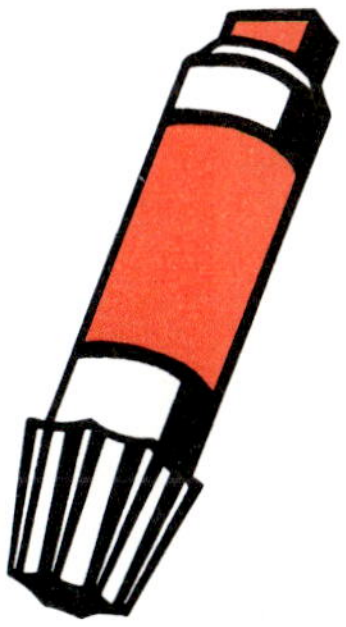

I. Spelling and Writing Read the paragraph. Use as many Spelling Words, Other Word Forms, and Challenge Words as you can to write *two* or more answers to each question. Proofread your work.

Walking is a good way to help you stay healthy and fit. When you walk, your heart beats more swiftly and your lungs fill deeply with air. You can begin walking regularly without hunting for expensive equipment and spending large sums of money. For the young or old, walking is a great way to enter the world of exercise.

1. What happens to your body when you walk?

   Example:

   When you walk, your heart beats more swiftly.

2. What makes walking a good form of exercise?

4

A. Pretest and Proofreading

B. Spelling Words and Phrases

1.	knee	bruised my knee
2.	knot	untied the knot
3.	knew	knew what to do
4.	knows	knows the way
5.	knife	the sharpest knife
6.	prize	first or second prize
7.	prices	high prices
8.	shine	the shine of new paint
9.	smile	made them smile
10.	slide	long, steep slide
11.	slid	slid across the ice
12.	slip	will slip on the playground
13.	grip	a firm grip
14.	spin	to spin in the air
15.	history	studied town history
16.	arithmetic	a page of arithmetic

Other Word Forms

knees, kneel
knots, knotted, knotting
know, known, knowing
knives, knifing
prizes
price
shines, shined, shining, shiny, shinier
smiled, smiling
slides, sliding, slider
slips, slipped, slippery
grips, gripping
spins, spinning, spun
histories, historical
arithmetical

C. Visual Warm-up Write each word in its correct shape.

a. b. c. d. e. f. g. h. i. j. k. l. m. n. o. p.

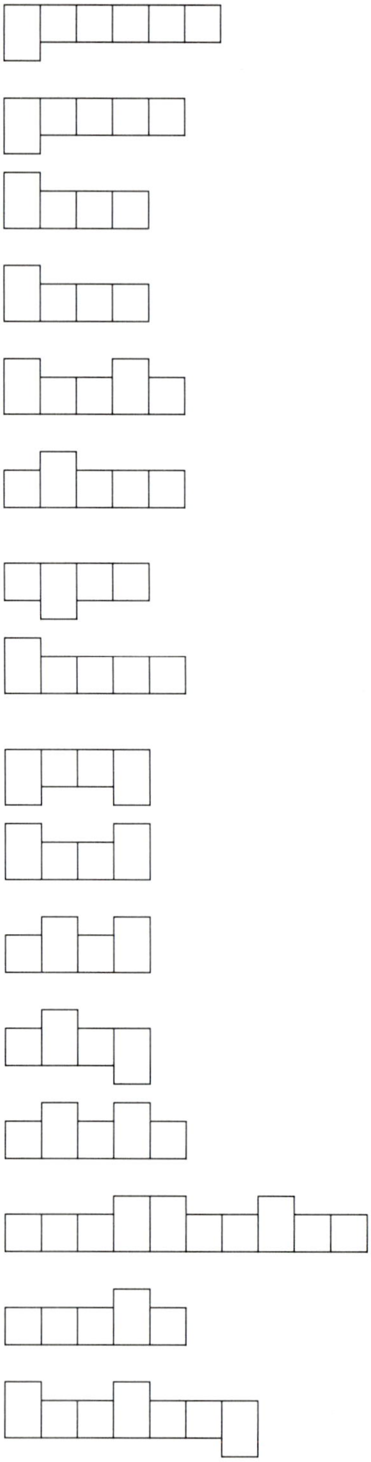

D. Be a Sentence Detective Complete the sentences with words from the spelling list. Write each word.

1. She once ________________ how to tie a ________________ .
2. She easily added the ________________ of the groceries because she was good at ________________ .
3. A lucky ________________ of the top will win the ________________ .
4. He ________________ the answer now that he has read his ________________ book.
5. On the playground be careful not to ________________ off the ________________ .
6. The butcher had a firm ________________ on the sharp ________________ .
7. Put a ________________ on your face and a ________________ on your shoes.
8. When she ________________ down the tree, she skinned her ________________ .

E. Sort Your Words Write each spelling word. A word may go under more than one heading.

Words with One Syllable	Words with Two, Three, or Four Syllables	Words with Silent *K*
1. ________________	14. ________________	17. ________________
2. ________________	15. ________________	18. ________________
3. ________________	16. ________________	19. ________________
4. ________________		20. ________________
5. ________________		21. ________________
6. ________________		
7. ________________		
8. ________________		
9. ________________		
10. ________________		
11. ________________		
12. ________________		
13. ________________		

Spelling Words

knee	knot	knew	knows	knife	prize
prices	shine	smile	slide	slid	slip
grip	spin	history	arithmetic		

F. Words and Meanings Write a spelling word for each meaning. Check your answers in the **Spelling Dictionary**.

1. was sure of the facts ________________
2. moved easily ________________
3. a record of past events ________________
4. a tight hold ________________
5. is sure of the facts ________________
6. a fastening made with string ________________
7. costs ________________
8. a leg joint ________________
9. brightness ________________
10. to move easily ________________
11. a sharp cutting tool ________________
12. a happy look on a person's face ________________
13. an award ________________
14. to slide suddenly without control ________________
15. adding and subtracting ________________
16. to turn around quickly ________________

G. Using Other Word Forms Write the Other Word Form that fits each clue.

Base Words: knee(l) history(es) knife(s) knot(ed) know(ing)

1. cutting tools ________________
2. lean on a knee ________________
3. understanding ________________
4. Civil War stories ________________
5. was tied together ________________

H. Challenge Words Write the Challenge Word that completes each sentence.

pirate	tissue	surprised	wives	simple

1. If it's easy, it's ________________ .
2. If it's thin paper, it may be ________________ .
3. If they're women, they may be ________________ .
4. If he's a buccaneer, he may be a ________________ .
5. If I'm stunned, I might be ________________ .

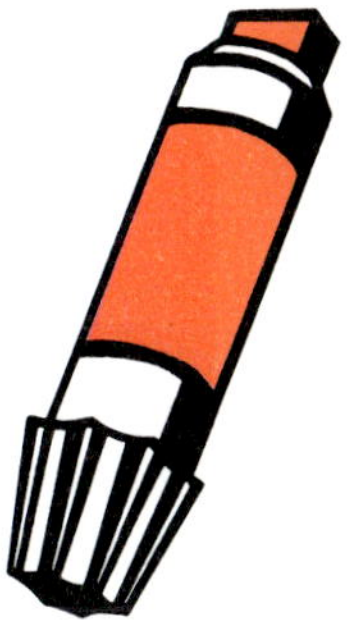

I. Spelling and Writing Write each set of words in a sentence. You may use Other Word Forms. Proofread your work.

1. history – grip
2. prices – prize
3. knife – knot
4. slid – knee
5. spin – shine
6. arithmetic – knows
7. smile – knew
8. slide – slip
9. simple – tissue
10. pirate – surprised
11. wives – smiled

5

A. Pretest and Proofreading

B. Spelling Words and Phrases

1.	**blade**	the skate blade
2.	**blame**	took all the blame
3.	**blaze**	sudden blaze
4.	**brave**	is brave to try
5.	**shake**	felt the earth shake
6.	**stake**	tied to a stake
7.	**skate**	only one roller skate
8.	**scale**	sang the scale
9.	**lend**	will lend the book
10.	**bend**	might bend the nail
11.	**melt**	saw it melt away
12.	**deck**	walked around the deck
13.	**flock**	gathered the flock
14.	**shock**	a shock from the lamp
15.	**blocks**	cement blocks
16.	**pocket**	jingled in my pocket

Other Word Forms

blades
blames, blamed, blaming
blazes, blazing
braver, bravest, bravely
shaky, shakes, shook, shaking
stakes, staked, staking
skates, skated, skating
scales
lends, lending
bends, bent, bending
melts, melted, melting
decks
flocks, flocked, flocking
shocks, shocked, shocking
block, blocked, blocking
pockets

C. Visual Warm-up

Write each word in its correct shape.

a.
b.
c.
d.
e.
f.
g.
h.
i.
j.
k.
l.
m.
n.
o.
p.

D. Hide and Seek The spelling words can be found in the word puzzle. The words appear across and down. Circle and write the words.

Across

1. ____________
2. ____________
3. ____________
4. ____________
5. ____________
6. ____________
7. ____________
8. ____________
9. ____________
10. ____________

r	m	o	t	b	l	o	c	k	s
t	e	u	b	l	a	m	e	a	p
a	l	b	l	a	z	e	t	b	o
m	t	r	n	d	e	c	k	l	c
s	h	a	k	e	t	r	e	e	k
k	f	v	m	p	b	e	n	d	e
a	l	e	s	c	a	l	e	l	t
t	o	l	e	n	d	r	e	c	o
e	c	s	t	a	k	e	t	e	n
f	k	o	e	s	h	o	c	k	a

Down

11. ____________
12. ____________
13. ____________
14. ____________
15. ____________
16. ____________

E. Finding Words The words in the spelling list appear in the beginning (A-H), middle (I-Q), or end (R-Z) of the **Spelling Dictionary**. Write each word.

Beginning A-H

1. ____________
2. ____________
3. ____________
4. ____________
5. ____________
6. ____________
7. ____________
8. ____________

Middle I-Q

9. ____________
10. ____________
11. ____________

End R-Z

12. ____________
13. ____________
14. ____________
15. ____________
16. ____________

Spelling Words

blade	blame	blaze	brave	shake	stake	skate
scale	lend	bend	melt	deck	flock	shock
blocks	pocket					

F. Sort Your Words

1. In alphabetical order, write the eight words ending with a silent *e*.

a. ____________ **d.** ____________ **g.** ____________

b. ____________ **e.** ____________ **h.** ____________

c. ____________ **f.** ____________

2. What does the silent *e* do to the vowel *a* in each word? ____________

____

3. Write the five words with *ck*.

____________ ____________ ____________

____________ ____________

4. Write the three spelling words you have not used on this page. Circle the final *lt* or *nd* in each word.

____________ ____________ ____________

G. Using Other Word Forms Write the Other Word Form that completes each sentence.

Base Words: blame(ed) brave(ly) blaze(ing) shake(ook) skate(ing)

1. Smooth ice is perfect for ________________ .
2. He was ________________ for the mistake.
3. The fire was ________________ through the forest.
4. She ________________ held the rearing horse.
5. She ________________ her head no.

H. Challenge Words Write the Challenge Word that replaces each underlined word or phrase.

flames	**gently**	**hollow**	**modern**	**watched**

1. Handle with care. ________________
2. We saw the movie. ________________
3. The fire may be out of control. ________________
4. That building is up-to-date. ________________
5. The tube is not solid. ________________

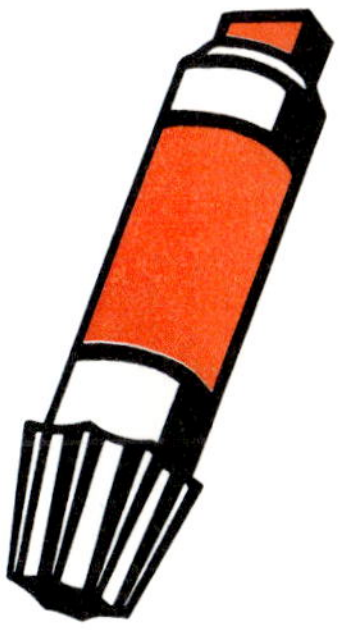

I. Spelling and Writing Read the story idea. Use the Spelling Words, Other Word Forms, and Challenge Words to help you think of an answer to each question. Proofread your work.

Story idea:
They looked up at the blazing sky.

1. What made them look up at the sky?
2. What caused the sky to blaze?
3. Who was looking at the sky?
4. Where were they?
5. How did they feel about what was happening?
6. What else was going on?

6

REVIEW

REVIEWING LESSONS 1-5

alike	blade	history	mile	sum
arithmetic	brave	hunter	pocket	swift
began	crossing	knee	seemed	tore
being	fate	knife	shake	woke

A. Break the Code Use the code to write an Other Word Form for each spelling word. Write each word.

a	b	c	d	e	f	g	h	i	j	k	l	m
↕	↕	↕	↕	↕	↕	↕	↕	↕	↕	↕	↕	↕
z	y	x	w	v	u	t	s	r	q	p	o	n

1. hfnh
2. hvvnrmt
3. uzgvw
4. yizevib
5. srhglirx
6. dzpvw
7. yv
8. pmrevh
9. hsllp
10. xilhhvw
11. zorpvmvhh
12. hdrugob
13. klxpvgufo
14. pmvvh
15. glim
16. nrovztv
17. yvtrm
18. sfmgvw
19. zirgsnvgrxzo
20. yozwvh

■	☆	▲	◆	●
cape	dive	races	pile	holes
mapping	rack	ax	lump	enter
cases	saves	blaze	smile	slip
spin	bend	shine	flock	stake

REVIEW

B. Words in a Series Use Other Word Forms to complete each series. The shapes tell you in what column you can find the spelling word. Use each Other Word Form only once.

1. jackets, coats, ■ ____________
2. heaps, loads, ◆ ____________
3. leaps, jumps, ☆ ____________
4. running, dashing, ▲ ____________
5. bars, poles, ☆ ____________
6. opening, pit, ● ____________
7. plan, chart, ■ ____________
8. tools, hatchets, ▲ ____________
9. bumps, chunks, ◆ ____________
10. came in, walked in, ● ____________
11. kept, stored, ☆ ____________
12. box, crate, ■ ____________
13. fell, tripped, ● ____________
14. grinning, laughing, ◆ ____________
15. burning, flaming, ▲ ____________
16. turning, circling, ■ ____________
17. curved, twisted, ☆ ____________
18. herds, packs, ◆ ____________
19. glowing, glaring, ▲ ____________
20. pegs, sticks, ● ____________

■	★	▲	◆	●
she's	size	he's	meet	won't
didn't	plum	prize	shock	slide
backward	melt	can't	across	lace
skate	knows	it's	grip	blame

REVIEW

C. Sentence Completion Write Other Word Forms or the spelling words to complete the sentences. The shapes tell you in what column you can find the spelling word. Write each word or its Other Word Form only once. If you need help, use the **Spelling Dictionary**.

1. We ● ________ be able to have a class ◆ ________ before the field trip.
2. Sometimes ▲ ________ not easy to ● ________ my sneakers.
3. We ■ ________ buy many ★ ________ at the grocery store.
4. I think ■ ________ wearing shoes that are two ★ ________ too big for her.
5. Are you sure ▲ ________ going to walk ◆ ________ the old bridge?
6. We ▲ ________ run ■ ________ without falling down.
7. I ★ ________ I can win one of the ▲ ________ at the fair.
8. We ◆ ________ the sides of the sled as we went ● ________ down the hill.
9. They couldn't go ■ ________ because the ice on the pond had ★ ________.
10. I was ◆ ________ when my cousin ● ________ me for eating all the cookies.

■	★	▲	◆	●
fade	madly	begun	knew	deck
dare	draft	lung	slid	scale
hire	camel	itself	knot	lend
wade	wore	begin	prices	blocks

D. Word Clues Write the spelling word that goes with each clue. The shape after each clue tells you in what column you can find the spelling word. Then write an Other Word Form for each spelling word. If you need help, use the **Spelling Dictionary**.

Word Clues	Spelling Words	Other Word Forms
1. a level on a ship ●	_ _ _ _	________
2. moved easily ◆	_ _ _ _	________
3. a challenge ■	_ _ _ _	________
4. to have had on ★	_ _ _ _	________
5. to start ▲	_ _ _ _ _	________
6. a flow of air ★	_ _ _ _ _	________
7. to give a loan ●	_ _ _ _	________
8. to pay for work ■	_ _ _ _	________
9. sure of the facts ◆	_ _ _ _	________
10. costs ◆	_ _ _ _ _ _	________
11. with great energy ★	_ _ _ _ _	________
12. for breathing air ▲	_ _ _ _	________
13. walk slowly into the water ■	_ _ _ _	________
14. a desert animal ★	_ _ _ _ _	________
15. a series of musical notes ●	_ _ _ _ _	________
16. rope tied together ◆	_ _ _ _	________
17. a pronoun ▲	_ _ _ _ _ _	
18. solid objects ●	_ _ _ _ _ _	________
19. to dim ■	_ _ _ _	________
20. already started ▲	_ _ _ _ _	________

REVIEW

7

A. Pretest and Proofreading

B. Spelling Words and Phrases

1.	drag	will drag it behind them
2.	snap	to snap the pencil
3.	trap	a harmless trap
4.	scrap	scrap of cloth
5.	bump	ran over a bump
6.	club	club meeting
7.	scrub	to scrub the floor
8.	hung	hung in the closet
9.	hungry	felt so hungry
10.	hundred	a hundred or more
11.	trust	honesty and trust
12.	brush	will brush their teeth
13.	bruise	a bruise on my elbow
14.	stocking	in their stocking feet
15.	unlock	to unlock the door
16.	o'clock	almost three o'clock

Other Word Forms

drags, dragged, dragging
snaps, snapped, snapping
traps, trapped, trapping
scraps
bumps, bumped, bumping
clubs
scrubs, scrubbed, scrubbing
hang, hangs, hanged, hanging
hunger, hungrier, hungriest
hundreds
trusts, trusted, trusting
brushes, brushed, brushing
bruises, bruised, bruising
stockings
unlocks, unlocked, unlocking

C. Visual Warm-up
Write each word in its correct shape.

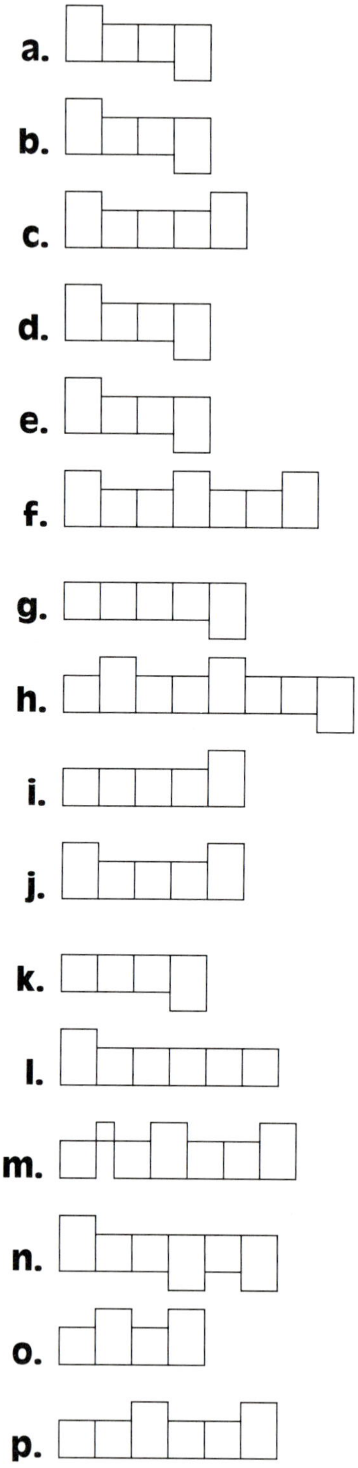

D. Hide and Seek The spelling words and some Other Word Forms (p. 28) can be found in the word puzzle. The words appear across and down. Circle and write the words.

h	o	t	r	a	p	b	r	u	s	h
u	c	h	u	n	d	r	e	d	c	u
n	l	u	n	b	r	u	s	s	r	n
g	o	n	l	r	a	i	n	c	u	g
r	c	g	o	u	g	s	a	r	b	s
i	k	e	c	i	d	e	p	u	u	t
e	b	r	k	s	r	m	p	b	m	o
s	u	t	d	i	a	e	i	b	p	c
t	m	r	r	n	g	s	n	i	o	k
s	p	a	a	g	g	c	g	n	c	i
n	e	p	g	p	e	r	c	g	l	n
a	d	s	s	i	d	a	h	o	u	g
p	c	l	u	b	t	p	e	r	b	v
h	u	n	g	r	y	t	r	u	s	t

Spelling Words
Across

1. ______
2. ______
3. ______
4. ______
5. ______
6. ______

Down

7. ______
8. ______
9. ______
10. ______
11. ______
12. ______
13. ______
14. ______
15. ______
16. ______

Other Word Forms
Down

17. ______
18. ______
19. ______
20. ______
21. ______
22. ______
23. ______
24. ______
25. ______
26. ______

E. Three in a Row Write a spelling word for the group it best fits.

1. black-and-blue, sore, ______
2. empty, wanting food, ______
3. attached, fastened, ______
4. racket, bat, ______
5. rub, wash, ______
6. lump, swelling, ______
7. paint, sweep, ______

Spelling Words

drag	snap	trap	scrap	bump	club
scrub	hung	hungry	hundred	trust	brush
bruise	stocking	unlock	o'clock		

F. Sort Your Words Each spelling word has two or more consonants together. Write each spelling word. A word may go in more than one column.

Beginning Consonants Together	Middle Consonants Together	End Consonants Together
1. ________	11. ________	16. ________
2. ________	12. ________	17. ________
3. ________	13. ________	18. ________
4. ________	14. ________	19. ________
5. ________	15. ________	20. ________
6. ________		21. ________
7. ________		22. ________
8. ________		
9. ________		
10. ________		

23. Write the four words that fit in two columns. ________

________ ________ ________

24. Write the word that fits in all three columns. ________

G. Using Other Word Forms Write the Other Word Form that fits each series.

Base Words: scrub(ing) bruise(ing) drag(ing) snap(ing) brush(ing)

1. snaps, snapped, ____________________

2. drags, dragged, ____________________

3. scrubs, scrubbed, ____________________

4. brushes, brushed, ____________________

5. bruises, bruised, ____________________

H. Challenge Words Write the Challenge Word that fits each group of words.

cottage	**sandal**	**throughout**	**sudden**	**taxes**

1. income, state, local, ____________________

2. hasty, without warning, quick, ____________________

3. leather, shoe, slipper, ____________________

4. everywhere, all over, everyplace, ____________________

5. house, cabin, lodge, ____________________

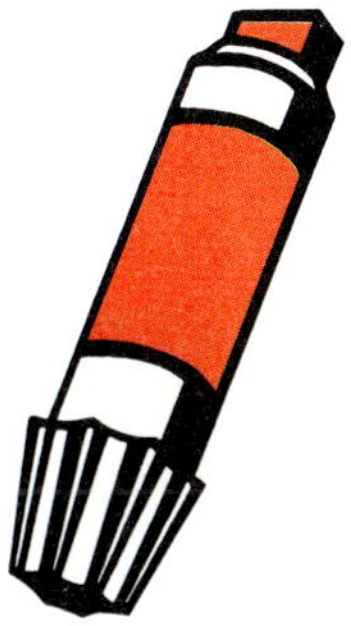

I. Spelling and Writing Write *two* or more answers to each question. Use as many Spelling Words, Other Word Forms, and Challenge Words as you can. A few words are suggested. Proofread your work.

1. What would you do if your new shoes hurt your feet?

snap – sandal – hung – hundred – stocking

Example: *I would hang the sandals in my closet and never wear them again.*

2. What would you do if your parents owned a beautiful summer home?

throughout – club – hungry – brush – cottage

3. What would you tell your friend if you damaged her new bicycle?

drag – bump – scrub – o'clock – sudden

8

A. Pretest and Proofreading

B. Spelling Words and Phrases

1. trim — a beard to trim
2. whip — crack of the whip
3. quit — will never quit
4. quite — not quite ready
5. tribe — peaceful tribe
6. pride — full of pride
7. crime — solved the crime
8. strike — to strike out
9. kept — kept apart
10. slept — slept soundly
11. fresh — fresh fish for sale
12. check — cashed a check
13. shell — shell on the beach
14. spend — to spend money
15. press — printing press
16. yellow — yellow ribbon

Other Word Forms

trims, trimmed, trimming
whips, whipped, whipping
quits, quitting, quitter
tribes, tribal
prides, prideful
crimes, criminal
strikes, striking, struck
keep, keeps, keeping, keeper
sleep, sleeps, sleeping, sleepy, sleepier, sleepiest
freshly, fresher, freshest
checks, checked, checking
shells, shelled, shelling
spends, spending, spent, spender
presses, pressed, pressing
yellows, yellowed

C. Visual Warm-up

Write each word in its correct shape.

a. b. c. d. e. f. g. h. i. j. k. l. m. n. o. p.

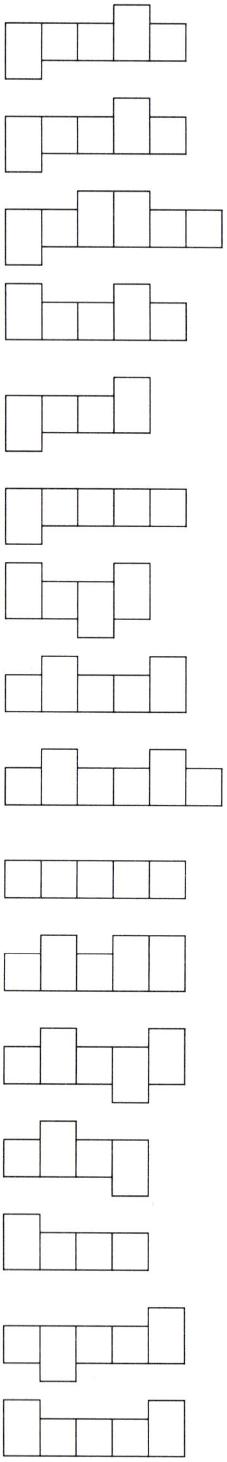

D. Missing Vowels Find the missing vowels and write the spelling words.

1. pr __ d __ ____________
2. q __ __ t __ ____________
3. k __ pt ____________
4. sh __ ll ____________
5. y __ ll __ w ____________
6. tr __ m ____________
7. fr __ sh ____________
8. pr __ ss ____________
9. wh __ p ____________
10. cr __ m __ ____________
11. q __ __ t ____________
12. ch __ ck ____________
13. sp __ nd ____________
14. tr __ b __ ____________
15. sl __ pt ____________
16. str __ k __ ____________

E. Scrambled Words Unscramble the scrambled word to find the spelling word that completes the sentence. Write the word.

1. We will ____________ (tuiq) working at five.
2. Buy some ____________ (shefr) milk for dinner.
3. Don't ____________ (ndesp) too much time in the sun.
4. She ____________ (ptsle) comfortably on the couch.
5. Don't try to ____________ (ikestr) the baseball too hard.
6. The ____________ (meicr) was committed at midnight.
7. Use these clippers to ____________ (mitr) the hedge.
8. Some animal once lived in this ____________ (lelsh).
9. ____________ (sespr) the strips of wood together.
10. He learned the language of the ____________ (ebitr).
11. She has always ____________ (ptek) this lucky coin.
12. We were ____________ (tequi) pleased to hear the good news.
13. Use blue paint and ____________ (lleyow) paint to make green.
14. Write your name on the ____________ (eckch).
15. ____________ (dipre) is the result of a job well done.
16. Use this spoon to ____________ (piwh) the cake batter.

Spelling Words

trim	whip	quit	quite	tribe	pride	crime
strike	kept	slept	fresh	check	shell	spend
press	yellow					

F. Words and Meanings Write a spelling word for each meaning. Check your answers in the **Spelling Dictionary**.

1. a bank order to pay money ____________________
2. a strap attached to a handle ____________________
3. to put force on something ____________________
4. to make neat by cutting ____________________
5. to give up ____________________
6. an unlawful action ____________________
7. to hit ____________________
8. rested ____________________
9. had for a long time ____________________
10. to pay out money ____________________
11. just made ____________________
12. a group of people ____________________
13. a hard covering on some animals ____________________
14. pleasure in one's actions ____________________
15. a color ____________________
16. completely ____________________

G. Using Other Word Forms Write the Other Word Form that completes each sentence.

Base Words: trim(ing) quit(er) crime(al) strike(uck) sleep(ing)

1. I keep trying so that I won't be called a ____________ .
2. He was ____________ very peacefully.
3. My mother is ____________ my hair.
4. The police officer led the ____________ to the jail.
5. The batter ____________ out.

H. Challenge Words Write the Challenge Word that completes each sentence.

dial	seventy	high school	shelves	widow

1. Once we turned a knob; now we turn a ____________ .
2. Once we stored them in boxes; now we store them on ____________ .
3. Once she was married; now she's a ____________ .
4. Once there were sixty; now there are ____________ .
5. Once they were in ____________ ; now they're in college.

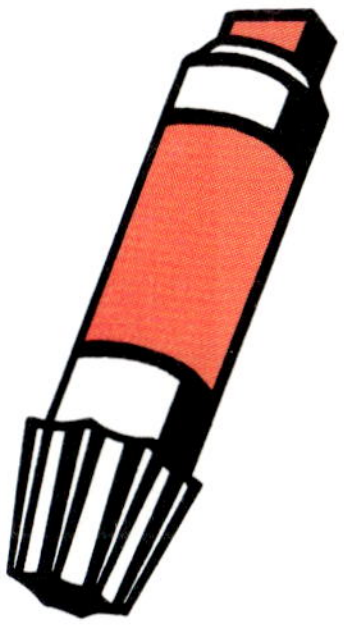

I. Spelling and Writing Read the paragraph. Use as many Spelling Words, Other Word Forms, and Challenge Words as you can to write *two* or more answers to each question. Proofread your work.

Dr. Margaret Mead was an anthropologist, a scientist who studies how different people live. For many years, Dr. Mead studied tribes of the Pacific Islands. She kept very careful records and checked to make sure that her information was correct. Dr. Mead wrote about such things as how the people ate, how they slept, and how they spent their time.

1. What are some of the things Dr. Mead did?
2. What might Dr. Mead have written about?

9

A. Pretest and Proofreading

B. Spelling Words and Phrases

1. sail	lowered the sail
2. jail	was put in jail
3. nails	hammered the nails
4. wait	if you wait
5. pain	pain in my neck
6. again	phoned once again
7. swim	learned to swim
8. thick	thick and thin
9. brick	the brick wall
10. trick	a magic trick
11. drill	the sound of the drill
12. skill	learned a new skill
13. loud	a long, loud cheer
14. proud	felt very proud
15. shout	a shout of joy
16. outfits	new camping outfits

Other Word Forms

sails, sailed, sailing, sailor
jails, jailed, jailer
nail, nailed, nailing
waits, waited, waiting, waiter
pains, painful
swims, swam, swimming
thicker, thickest, thickly
bricks
tricks, tricky, trickier, trickiest
drills, drilled, drilling
skills, skillful, skillfully, skilled
louder, loudest, loudly
proudly, prouder, proudest
shouts, shouted, shouting
outfit, outfitted, outfitting

C. Visual Warm-up

Write each word in its correct shape.

a. 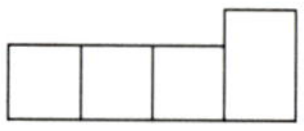

b. 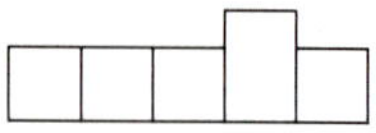

c. 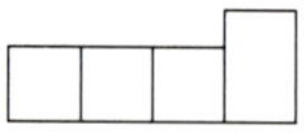

d. 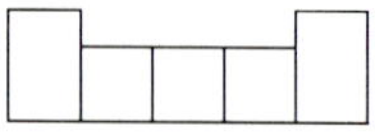

e. 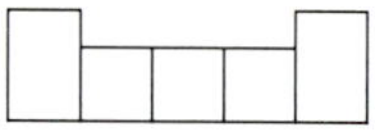

f. 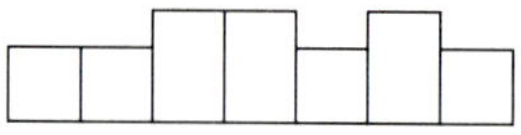

g. 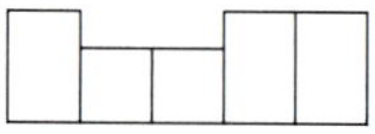

h. 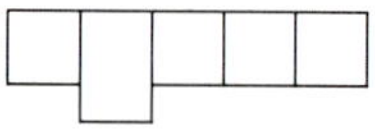

i. 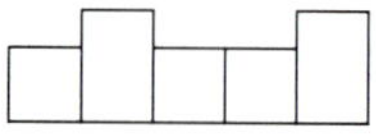

j. 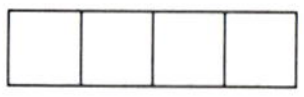

k. 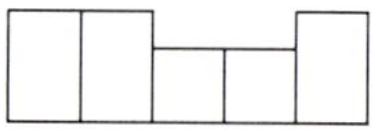

l. 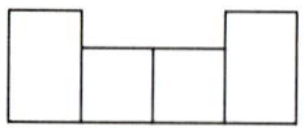

m. 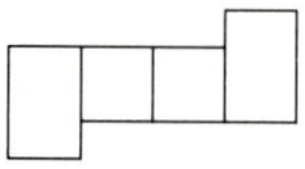

n. 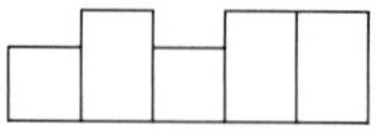

o. 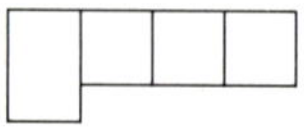

p. 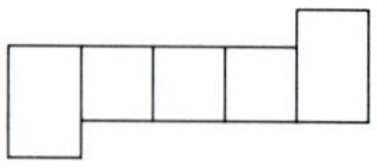

D. Sort Your Words

1. Write the spelling words in groups that rhyme.

a. ____________________
b. ____________________

c. ____________________
d. ____________________

e. ____________________
f. ____________________
g. ____________________

h. ____________________
i. ____________________

2. Write the seven spelling words that did not fit into a rhyming group. Put a check beside the compound word.

____________________ ____________________
____________________ ____________________
____________________ ____________________
____

E. Word Search

The spelling words can be found in the word puzzle. The words appear across and down. Circle and write the words.

s	a	i	l	b	p	a	i	n
h	e	s	p	r	o	u	d	o
o	u	t	f	i	t	s	w	e
u	n	r	o	c	d	k	a	t
t	h	i	c	k	r	i	i	s
a	l	c	m	s	i	l	t	s
g	o	k	s	w	l	l	m	n
a	s	j	a	i	l	o	u	d
i	n	t	o	m	e	t	s	y
n	a	i	l	s	t	p	o	e

Across

1. ____________________
2. ____________________
3. ____________________
4. ____________________
5. ____________________
6. ____________________
7. ____________________
8. ____________________

Down

9. ____________________
10. ____________________
11. ____________________
12. ____________________
13. ____________________
14. ____________________
15. ____________________
16. ____________________

Spelling Words

sail	jail	nails	wait	pain	again	swim
thick	brick	trick	drill	skill	loud	proud
shout	outfits					

F. Words and Meanings Write a spelling word for each meaning. Check your answers in the **Spelling Dictionary**.

1. pointed metal pieces that hold things together ________________
2. material that catches wind on a boat ________________
3. to move in water with arms and legs ________________
4. a place where lawbreakers are kept ________________
5. the ability to do something well ________________
6. a tool for making holes ________________
7. a block of baked clay ________________
8. feeling very pleased ________________
9. to stay in a place ________________
10. sets of equipment ________________
11. one more time ________________
12. a clever act ________________
13. a loud cry ________________
14. not quiet ________________
15. not thin ________________
16. hurt ________________

G. Using Other Word Forms Write the Other Word Form that fits each clue.

Base Words: sail(or) tricky(er) swim(ing) outfit(ed) pain(ful)

1. more clever ______________

2. doing laps in a pool ______________

3. describes a broken leg ______________

4. naval person ______________

5. dressed up ______________

H. Challenge Words Write the Challenge Words to complete the short story.

amazement	**waited**	**finished**	**downtown**	**railroad**

On our way **(1.)** ______________ we crossed over the **(2.)** ______________ tracks. To our **(3.)** ______________, we heard a loud, strange whistle. When the sound **(4.)** ______________, we **(5.)** ______________ to see the train that made such an eerie sound. No train came, however.

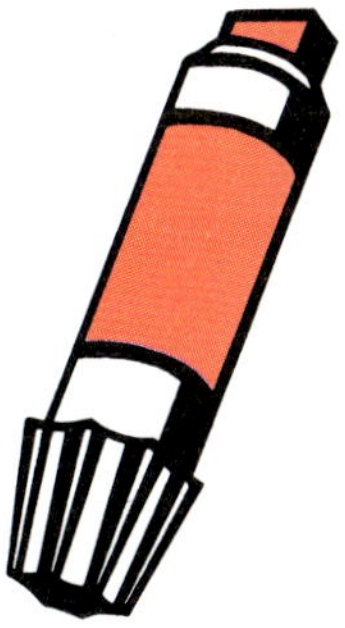

I. Spelling and Writing Read the paragraph. Use as many Spelling Words, Other Word Forms, and Challenge Words as you can to write *two* or more answers to each question. Proofread your work.

In the downtown area of many cities, skilled workers make new buildings out of old, empty ones. An old railroad station can be made into a shopping mall. Closed factories can be turned into new homes. Besides changing a building, workers sometimes use materials from buildings that are being torn down. For example, bricks from the thick walls of a torn-down jail can be used again to build something new. People who live in the cities are often amazed when they see the finished buildings.

1. How can old buildings be used to make new ones?

2. How do you think people feel when the buildings are completed?

10

A. Pretest and Proofreading

B. Spelling Words and Phrases

1.	chase	a dangerous chase
2.	space	far into space
3.	trace	a trace of smoke
4.	scrape	to scrape the plate
5.	frame	the picture frame
6.	shame	a shame to miss the parade
7.	share	a share of the dessert
8.	gown	white wedding gown
9.	clown	a clown with big feet
10.	power	power tools
11.	tower	tall steel tower
12.	shower	cold shower
13.	crowd	a crowd at the game
14.	homesick	homesick camper
15.	notebooks	notebooks for school
16.	sore	sore toe

Other Word Forms

chases, chased chasing
spaces, spaced, spacing
traces, traced, tracing
scrapes, scraped, scraping
frames
shames, shameful, shamed, shaming
shares, shared, sharing
gowns
clowns, clowning
powers, powerful
towers, towered, towering
showers, showered, showering
crowds, crowded
homesickness
notebook
sorely, sorer, sorest

C. Visual Warm-up

Write each word in its correct shape.

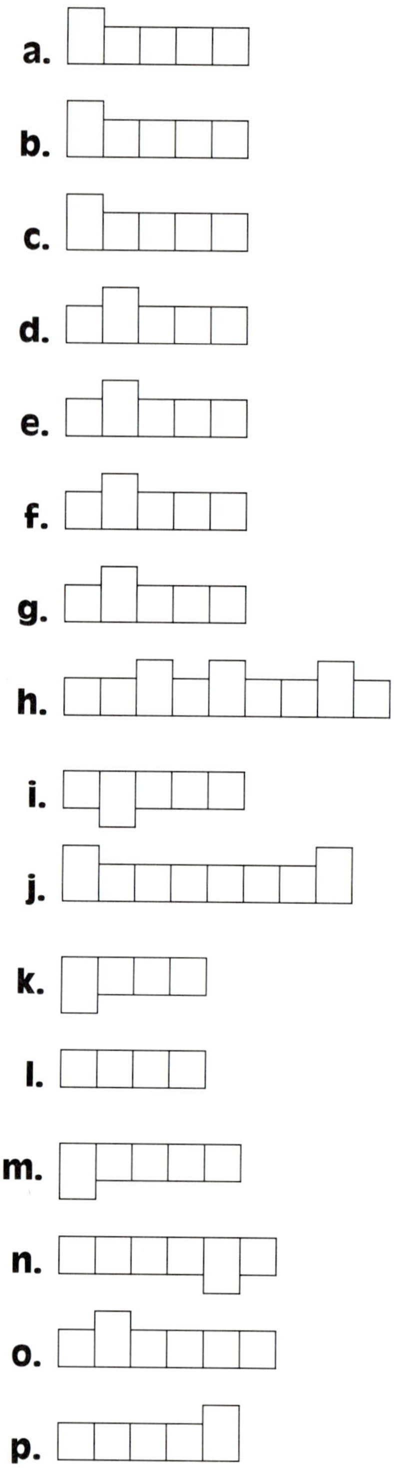

D. Finding Words The words in the spelling list appear in the beginning (A-H), middle (I-Q), or end (R-Z) of the **Spelling Dictionary**. Write each word.

Beginning A-H	Middle I-Q	End R-Z
1. ______	7. ______	9. ______
2. ______	8. ______	10. ______
3. ______		11. ______
4. ______		12. ______
5. ______		13. ______
6. ______		14. ______
		15. ______
		16. ______

E. Sort Your Words Write each spelling word. Beside each word write an Other Word Form (p. 40).

Words with *ow*	Other Word Forms	Words with a Long *a*	Other Word Forms
1. ______	______	10. ______	______
2. ______	______	11. ______	______
3. ______	______	12. ______	______
4. ______	______	13. ______	______
5. ______	______	14. ______	______
6. ______	______	15. ______	______

Words with *sh*	Other Word Forms	Words with a Long *o*	Other Word Forms
7. ______	______	16. ______	______
8. ______	______	17. ______	______
9. ______	______		

18. Write the two words that fit under more than one heading. ______ ______

19. Write the word that does not fit under any heading. ______

Spelling Words

chase	space	trace	scrape	frame	shame
share	gown	clown	power	tower	shower
crowd	homesick	notebooks	sore		

F. Name the Book Write a spelling word for each clue. Then join the boxed letters and write the title of a famous storybook.

1. what a ____ — _ _ _ [ ] _
2. painful — _ [ ] _ _
3. to draw over — [ ] _ _ _ _
4. to divide into parts — _ [ ] _ _ _
5. rain — _ _ _ _ [ ] _
6. a picture ____ — _ [ ] _ _ _
7. dress — [ ] _ _ _
8. lots of people — _ _ [ ] _ _
9. a tall, slender building — _ [ ] _ _ _
10. to rub off — [ ] _ _ _ _ _
11. to run after — _ _ _ _ [ ]
12. school supplies — _ _ [ ] _ _ _ _ _ _
13. an open area — _ _ [ ] _ _
14. a joker — _ [ ] _ _ _
15. strength — _ _ _ [ ] _
16. missing one's home — _ _ _ _ [ ] _ _ _
17. Write the name of the famous storybook. __________ __________ __________

G. Using Other Word Forms Add an ending to each word to write an Other Word Form.

1. chase + ing = ________________
2. space + ing = ________________
3. trace + ing = ________________
4. scrape + ing = ________________
5. share + ing = ________________
6. What letter keeps disappearing? ________________

H. Challenge Words Write the Challenge Word that completes each sentence.

chores	compared	coward	enclosed	frowned

1. The payment is ________________ in the envelope.
2. The children finished their ________________ .
3. Do you expect a ________________ to be the hero?
4. The clown both smiled and ________________ throughout his act.
5. ________________ to yesterday, it's hot today.

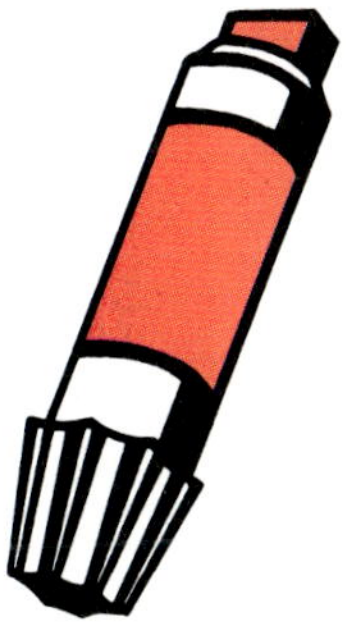

I. Spelling and Writing Write each set of words in a sentence. You may use Other Word Forms. Proofread your work.

1. homesick – crowd
2. scrape – sore
3. shower – power
4. tower – space
5. frame – share
6. shame – clown
7. notebooks – trace
8. chase – gown
9. chores – compared
10. coward – frowned
11. enclosed – notebook

11

A. Pretest and Proofreading

B. Spelling Words and Phrases

1.	mild	mild weather
2.	bind	to bind the book
3.	blind	a blind corner
4.	climb	whenever they climb
5.	higher	the higher of the two flags
6.	highest	the highest mountain
7.	highway	the longest highway
8.	mighty	a mighty roar
9.	post	fence post
10.	mostly	mostly in the morning
11.	almost	almost there
12.	sort	some sort of game
13.	sword	a dull, broad sword
14.	worn	worn only in winter
15.	worth	our money's worth
16.	worry	nothing to worry about

Other Word Forms

milder, mildest, mildly
binds, binder, binding, bound
blinds, blinded, blinding, blindly
climbs, climbed, climbing
high, highly
highways
might, mightier, mightiest
posts, posted, posting
much, more, most
sorts, sorted, sorting
swords
wear, wore, wearing
worthless, worthy
worries, worried, worrying

C. Visual Warm-up

Write each word in its correct shape.

a. 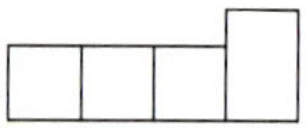

b. 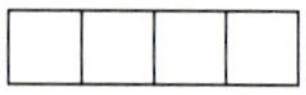

c. 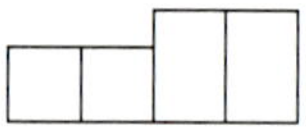

d. 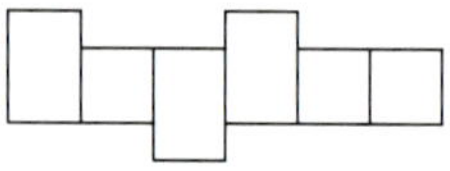

e. 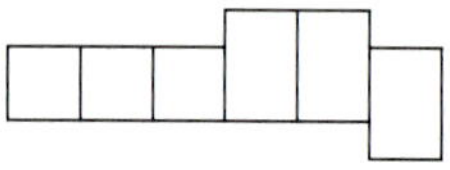

f. 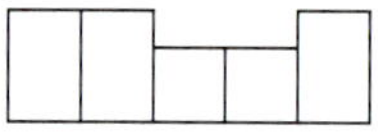

g. 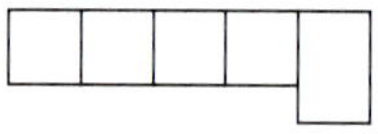

h. 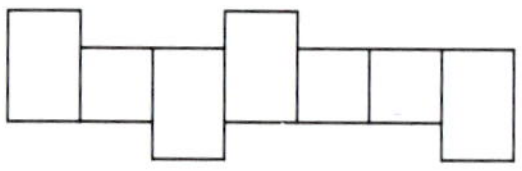

i. 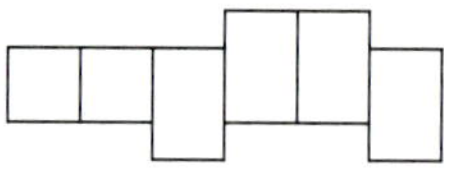

j. 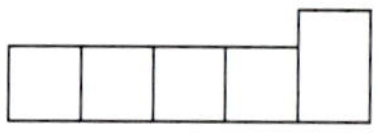

k. 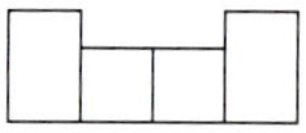

l. 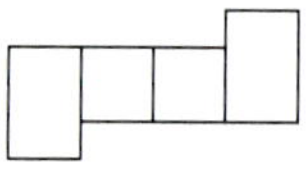

m. 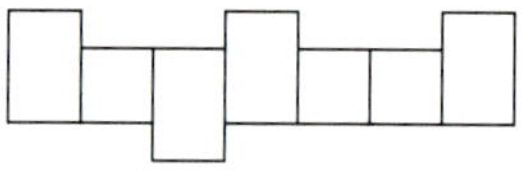

n. 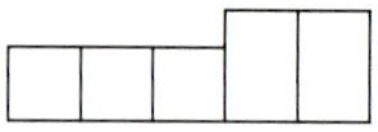

o. 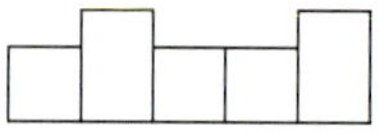

p. 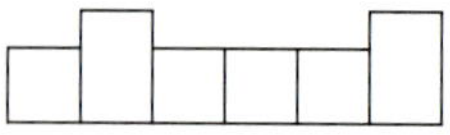

D. All in a Row Write the sixteen spelling words in alphabetical order. Then join the boxed letters and write four hidden words.

1. __ __ [ ] __ __ __
2. __ [ ] __ __
3. __ [ ] __ __ __
4. __ [ ] __ __ __
5. Hidden Word: ______________
6. __ __ __ [ ] __ __
7. __ [ ] __ __ __ __ __
8. __ __ [ ] __ __ __ __
9. __ __ __ [ ] __ __
10. Hidden Word: ______________
11. __ __ [ ] __
12. __ [ ] __ __ __ __
13. __ __ [ ] __
14. __ __ __ [ ]
15. Hidden Word: ______________
16. __ __ __ __ [ ]
17. __ [ ] __ __
18. __ [ ] __ __ __
19. __ __ [ ] __ __
20. Hidden Word: ______________

E. Base Words The spelling list contains eleven base words and five words that are not base words. Write each spelling word.

Words That Are Not Base Words	Base Words
1. worthy	______________
2. worrying	______________
3. highways	______________
4. mildly	______________
5. swords	______________
6. posted	______________
7. binder	______________
8. climbing	______________
9. blindly	______________
10. sorting	______________
11. ______________	high
12. ______________	high
13. ______________	might
14. ______________	wear
15. ______________	much

16. Write the one base word not used above. ______________

Spelling Words

mild	bind	blind	climb	higher	highest
highway	mighty	post	mostly	almost	sort
sword	worn	worth	worry		

F. Three in a Row Write a spelling word for the group it best fits.

1. feel troubled, be uneasy, ____________________
2. hidden, not seeing, ____________________
3. nearly, close to, ____________________
4. not hot, not cold, ____________________
5. value, importance, ____________________
6. kind, type, ____________________
7. ragged, damaged, ____________________
8. tie together, glue, ____________________
9. wood marker, fence, holder, ____________________
10. mainly, for the most part, ____________________

G. Using Other Word Forms Write the Other Word Form that completes each phrase.

Base Words: bind(ing) mighty(er) worth(less) climb(ing) mild(ly)

1. not strongly, but ______________
2. not valuable, but ______________
3. not untying, but ______________
4. not falling, but ______________
5. not weaker, but ______________

H. Challenge Words Write the Challenge Word that fits each group of words.

cords	**blindfold**	**bride**	**throat**	**scarecrow**

1. marry, vows, groom, ______________
2. handkerchief, eyes, cover, ______________
3. knotted, string, ropes, ______________
4. frighten, birds, cornfield, ______________
5. voice box, swallow, choke, ______________

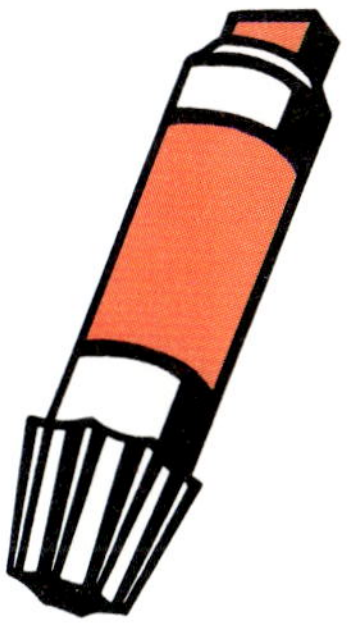

I. Spelling and Writing Read the story idea. Use the Spelling Words, Other Word Forms, and Challenge Words to help you think of an answer to each question. Proofread your work.

Story idea:
The car stopped suddenly in the middle of a busy highway.

1. Who was in the car?
2. Where was the car going?
3. Why did the car stop suddenly?
4. What were the weather and traffic like?
5. What did drivers of the other cars do?
6. When did this happen?

12 REVIEWING LESSONS 7-11

bruise	hung	outfits	proud	thick
crime	hungry	pain	quit	unlock
higher	kept	power	shame	worry
homesick	mighty	pride	sore	worth

REVIEW

A. Hide and Seek Twenty Other Word Forms can be found in the word puzzle. The words appear across and down. Circle and write each word. If you need help, use the **Spelling Dictionary**.

t	h	i	c	k	e	r	b	s	h	a	m	e	d	q
h	u	n	g	r	i	e	r	x	s	o	r	e	l	y
a	m	p	a	i	n	f	u	l	n	e	u	t	z	s
n	c	f	k	l	r	q	i	n	h	g	n	p	v	w
g	k	e	e	p	t	u	s	o	a	b	l	e	h	o
w	i	z	a	o	r	i	e	p	p	o	o	s	l	r
h	b	c	d	w	f	t	d	r	r	i	c	p	a	r
c	t	h	g	e	s	s	u	i	o	r	k	c	d	i
r	w	j	o	r	e	f	w	d	u	b	e	h	o	e
i	o	u	t	f	i	t	z	e	d	o	d	i	t	d
m	r	v	n	u	l	d	o	s	l	y	v	g	r	e
i	t	a	b	l	c	h	k	p	y	s	c	h	w	a
n	h	z	h	o	m	e	s	i	c	k	n	e	s	s
a	y	e	r	u	k	n	t	b	m	o	v	s	i	r
l	m	i	g	h	t	i	e	r	u	e	j	t	l	n

Across

1.

2.

3.

4.

5.

6.

7.

8.

9.

Down

10.

11.

12.

13.

14.

15.

16.

17.

18.

19.

20.

trap	tribe	trick	scrape	sort
trust	trim	sail	gown	post
hundred	press	jail	crowd	brick
brush	check	drill	tower	blind

B. Word Operations Use words from the spelling list to complete the exercises below. If you need help, use the **Spelling Dictionary**.

Operation Past Tense Write the *ed* form of each word.

1. trust *trusted*
2. blind ____
3. post ____
4. tower ____
5. press ____
6. check ____
7. trick ____
8. crowd ____
9. drill ____
10. brush ____

Operation Plural Write the *s* form of each word.

11. sort *sorts*
12. hundred ____
13. trim ____
14. jail ____
15. gown ____
16. scrape ____
17. brick ____
18. sail ____
19. trap ____
20. tribe ____

REVIEW

■	☆	▲	◆	●
bind	club	nails	shower	swim
chase	drag	scrub	slept	sword
climb	highest	share	snap	wait
clown	highway	shell	strike	whip

C. Word Clues Write the spelling word that goes with each clue. The shape after each clue tells you in what column you can find the spelling word. Then write an Other Word Form for each spelling word. If you need help, use the **Spelling Dictionary**.

REVIEW

Word Clues	Spelling Words	Other Word Forms
1. to make a sharp sound ◆	___ ___ ___ ___	________
2. to rub clean ▲	___ ___ ___ ___ ___	________
3. to pull along slowly ☆	___ ___ ___ ___	________
4. a group of people who meet ☆	___ ___ ___ ___	________
5. a hard outer covering ▲	___ ___ ___ ___ ___	________
6. to hit ◆	___ ___ ___ ___ ___ ___	________
7. a strap on a handle ●	___ ___ ___ ___	________
8. rested ◆	___ ___ ___ ___ ___	________
9. pointed pieces of metal ▲	___ ___ ___ ___ ___	________
10. to move in water ●	___ ___ ___ ___	________
11. to tie together ■	___ ___ ___ ___	________
12. to stay in a place ●	___ ___ ___ ___	________
13. a funny circus person ■	___ ___ ___ ___ ___	________
14. a bath of spraying water ◆	___ ___ ___ ___ ___ ___	________
15. to use with others ▲	___ ___ ___ ___ ___	________
16. a sharp weapon ●	___ ___ ___ ___ ___	________
17. to move upward ■	___ ___ ___ ___ ___	________
18. tallest ☆	___ ___ ___ ___ ___ ___ ___	________
19. a main road ☆	___ ___ ___ ___ ___ ___ ___	________
20. to run after ■	___ ___ ___ ___ ___	________

■	★	▲	◆	●
bump	spend	shout	notebooks	mostly
o'clock	quite	loud	frame	almost
stocking	fresh	skill	trace	mild
scrap	yellow	again	space	worn

D. Sentences in Paragraphs Write Other Word Forms or the spelling words to complete the sentences. Use the words from the first column to complete the first paragraph, and so on. The shapes will help you match the columns with the paragraphs. Write each word or its Other Word Form only once. If you need help, use the **Spelling Dictionary**.

■ At one **(1.)** __ __ __ __ __ __ in the morning, I crept downstairs in my **(2.)** __ __ __ __ __ __ __ __ feet to the refrigerator. Quietly, I opened the door to see if any **(3.)** __ __ __ __ __ __ of food were there. While reaching for the cheese, I **(4.)** __ __ __ __ __ __ my head and wished I had stayed in bed.

★ In the garden shop, we saw lovely **(5.)** __ __ __ __ __ __ flowers that had been **(6.)** __ __ __ __ __ __ __ cut. They were **(7.)** __ __ __ __ __ beautiful, but we couldn't buy any because we had **(8.)** __ __ __ __ __ all of our money at the movies.

▲ Once **(9.)** __ __ __ __ __ our voices got **(10.)** __ __ __ __ __ __ as we **(11.)** __ __ __ __ __ __ __ and laughed during the math game. Our teacher was pleased to see us using the new **(12.)** __ __ __ __ __ __ we had learned.

◆ I wanted to make a picture **(13.)** __ __ __ __ __ for a drawing I had **(14.)** __ __ __ __ __ __ in my art **(15.)** __ __ __ __ __ __ __ __ . I had no wood for a real frame. I cut some blue paper and **(16.)** __ __ __ __ __ __ it evenly around my drawing to make a border.

● It is **(17.)** __ __ __ __ __ __ spring, and the **(18.)** __ __ __ __ __ __ weather is coming. I have to **(19.)** __ __ __ __ a coat **(20.)** __ __ __ __ often in the morning when I walk to school.

REVIEW

13

A. Pretest and Proofreading

B. Spelling Words and Phrases

1.	**bid**	will bid at the auction
2.	**dim**	to dim the lights
3.	**tin**	made of tin
4.	**mix**	to mix and pour
5.	**sixth**	sixth time
6.	**sixteen**	sixteen steps to the door
7.	**mint**	flavor of mint
8.	**mist**	hidden in the mist
9.	**ticket**	movie ticket
10.	**chart**	a temperature chart
11.	**March**	a windy March
12.	**marble**	marble floors
13.	**marker**	a red marker
14.	**farther**	farther away
15.	**reward**	collected the reward
16.	**plane**	taking a plane
17.	**replace**	will replace the book
18.	**skating**	skating party

Other Word Forms

bids, bidding, bidder
dims, dimmed, dimming, dimmer, dimmest, dimly
tins, tinned
mixes, mixed, mixing, mixer
six, sixths
sixteenth
mints, minted, minting
mists, misted, misting, misty
tickets, ticketed, ticketing
charts, charted, charting
Mar.
marbles, marbled, marbling
mark, marks, marked, marking
far, farthest
rewards, rewarded, rewarding
planes
replaces, replaced, replacing
skate, skated, skater

C. Visual Warm-up

Write each word in its correct shape.

a. 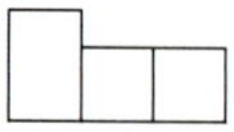

b. 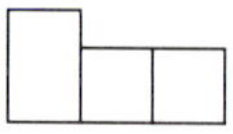

c. 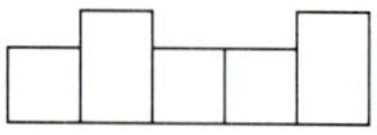

d. 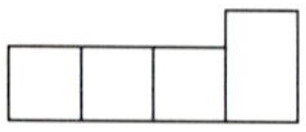

e. 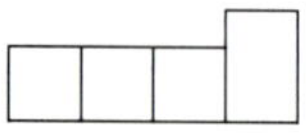

f. 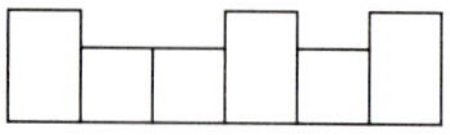

g. 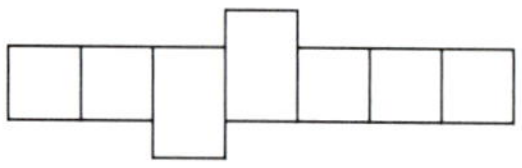

h. 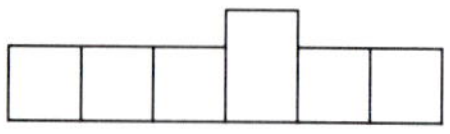

i. 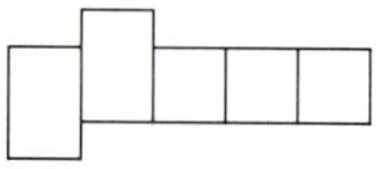

j. 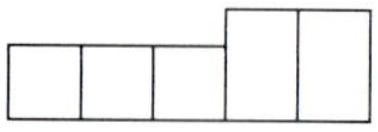

k. 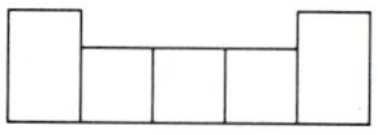

l. 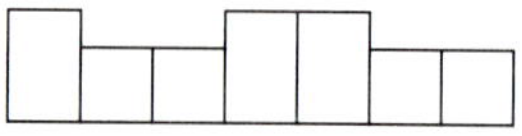

m. 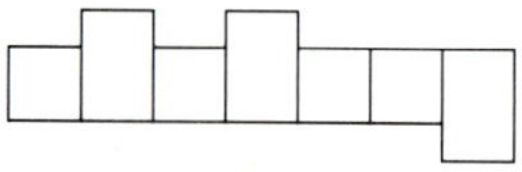

n. 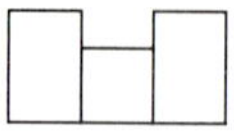

o. 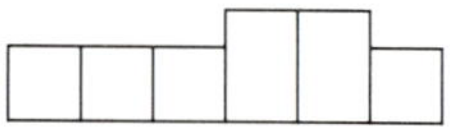

p. 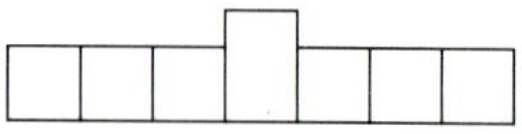

q. 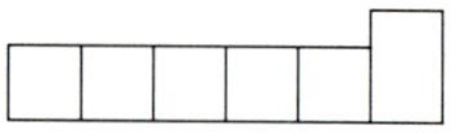

r. 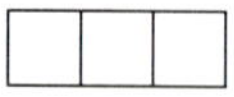

D. Word Match-ups Find a word in the spelling list that best fits each phrase. Write each word. Check your answers in the **Spelling Dictionary**.

1. a winter sport ________
2. to stir together ________
3. flies in the air ________
4. the third month ________
5. twelve plus four ________
6. a crayon ________
7. light rain ________
8. a flavorful plant ________
9. before the seventh ________
10. not nearer ________
11. to make an offer ________
12. a round glass toy ________
13. to make darker ________
14. to fill the place of ________
15. metal for cans ________
16. a movie pass ________
17. a prize ________
18. a map ________

E. All in a Row Write the eighteen spelling words in alphabetical order. Then join the boxed letters and write four hidden words.

1. □ _ _
2. _ _ □ _ _
3. _ □ _
4. _ _ _ □ _ _ _
5. Hidden Word: ________
6. _ _ _ □ _ _
7. _ □ _ _ _
8. _ _ □ _ _ _
9. _ _ □ _
10. _ _ □ _
11. Hidden Word: ________
12. □ _ _
13. _ _ □ _ _
14. _ _ _ □ _ _ _
15. _ □ _ _ _ _
16. Hidden Word: ________
17. □ _ _ _ _ _ _
18. _ _ _ □ _
19. _ _ □ _ _ _ _
20. _ □ _ _ _ _
21. _ _ □
22. Hidden Word: ________

Spelling Words

bid	dim	tin	mix	sixth	sixteen
mint	mist	ticket	chart	March	marble
marker	farther	reward	plane	replace	skating

F. Solve the Puzzle Solve the puzzle by using words from the spelling list. Write each word. Check your answers in the **Spelling Dictionary**.

Across

3. money given for information
7. after the fifth
8. something that holds your place
9. a round plaything
11. to offer to pay a certain price
12. a tag or label
13. to stir
14. a plant used for flavoring

Down

1. aircraft
2. a graph or map
3. to take the place of
4. not bright
5. at a greater distance
6. a month
7. gliding on ice
10. eight plus eight
12. a silvery metal
13. a bath of spraying water

G. Using Other Word Forms Write the Other Word Form that completes each sentence.

Base Words: mist(y) mix(ed) bid(ing) dim(er) replace(ing)

1. They were ____________ the old wallpaper.
2. Because of the light rain, it was a ____________ morning.
3. As the sun set, it grew ____________ in the woods.
4. The vegetables in the salad were ____________ together.
5. They were not ____________ at the auction.

H. Challenge Words Write the Challenge Word that completes each phrase.

labels	**fifteen**	**cartons**	**harness**	**spacecraft**

1. either boxes or ____________
2. either an airplane or a ____________
3. either fourteen or ____________
4. either a leash or a ____________
5. either tags or ____________

I. Spelling and Writing Write each set of words in a sentence. You may use Other Word Forms. Proofread your work.

1. bid – ticket
2. plane – mist
3. sixth – March
4. marble – reward
5. marker – chart
6. farther – sixteen
7. mix – mint
8. dim – replace
9. tin – skating
10. labels – cartons
11. fifteen – spacecraft
12. harness – replaced

14

A. Pretest and Proofreading

B. Spelling Words and Phrases

1.	**oil**	motor oil
2.	**boil**	will boil the water
3.	**soil**	dark, wet soil
4.	**join**	if they join us
5.	**coin**	flipped a coin
6.	**noise**	a sudden noise
7.	**point**	point of the story
8.	**sliced**	sliced tomatoes
9.	**sliding**	a sliding door
10.	**driving**	driving carefully
11.	**shining**	shining the floor
12.	**writer**	sky writer
13.	**river**	a winding river
14.	**deliver**	a load to deliver
15.	**silver**	silver and gold
16.	**women**	several women
17.	**Wednesday**	next Wednesday
18.	**September**	the first of September

Other Word Forms

oils, oiled, oiling, oily
boils, boiled, boiling, boiler
soils, soiled, soiling
joins, joined, joining
coins, coined, coining
noisy, noisier, noisiest, noisily
points, pointed, pointing, pointer
slice, slices, slicing, slicer
slide, slid, slider
drive, drives, drove
shine, shines, shone, shined, shiny
write, writes, wrote, writing, written
rivers
delivers, delivered, delivering, delivery
silvery
woman, womanly
Wed.
Sept.

C. Visual Warm-up

Write each word in its correct shape.

a. b. c. d. e. f. g. h. i. j. k. l. m. n. o. p. q. r.

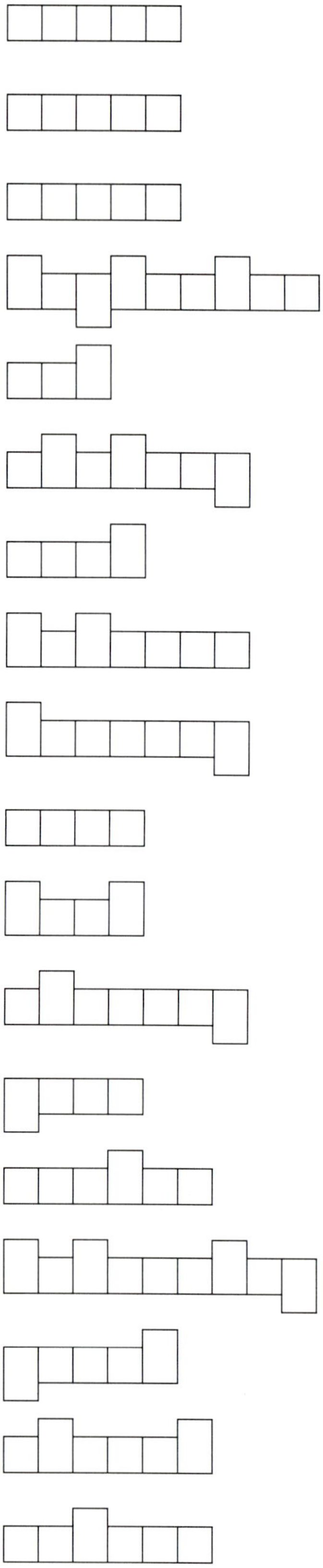

D. Sort Your Words Write the spelling words under the correct headings. Check your answers in the **Spelling Dictionary**. You will have two words left over.

Words with a Short *i* Sound	Words with a Long *i* Sound	Words with an *oi* Sound
1. ______	5. ______	10. ______
2. ______	6. ______	11. ______
3. ______	7. ______	12. ______
4. ______	8. ______	13. ______
	9. ______	14. ______
		15. ______
		16. ______

17. Write the two leftover words. ______ ______

E. Word Operations As a word doctor, you must change some words before adding a suffix. Make the changes that are needed and write the new words. Some words will not need a change.

Word	Suffix	New Word
1. boil	er	______
2. join	ing	______
3. write	er	______
4. deliver	ing	______
5. slice	ed	______
6. point	ed	______
7. drive	ing	______
8. soil	ed	______
9. shine	ing	______
10. oil	ing	______
11. slide	ing	______
12. coin	ed	______

Spelling Words

oil	boil	soil	join	coin
noise	point	sliced	sliding	driving
shining	writer	river	deliver	silver
women	Wednesday	September		

F. Word Swap Use the spelling words and Other Word Forms (p. 56) to replace the underlined words or phrases. Write the words.

On the second **(1.)** Tuesday of **(2.)** January, six **(3.)** men stepped into the **(4.)** sparkling bus. The conductor **(5.)** aimed his fingers at a box and asked the people to put their **(6.)** whitish **(7.)** dimes into it. There was so much **(8.)** loud sound that the driver stopped **(9.)** making the bus move. The bus began **(10.)** skidding on a puddle of **(11.)** slime and just missed going into a **(12.)** lake. A **(13.)** person who makes up stories was on his way to **(14.)** bring his story to town. He **(15.)** got together with some people from the bus. One woman showed him the **(16.)** dirt they had landed in. Then she dropped her package of **(17.)** cooked, **(18.)** carved meat. The bus was soon towed.

1. ____________ **7.** ____________ **13.** ____________

2. ____________ **8.** ____________ **14.** ____________

3. ____________ **9.** ____________ **15.** ____________

4. ____________ **10.** ____________ **16.** ____________

5. ____________ **11.** ____________ **17.** ____________

6. ____________ **12.** ____________ **18.** ____________

G. Be a Word Detective The same two vowels are missing from each of the words below. Write the words.

1. s __ __ l ____________

2. b __ __ l ____________

3. p __ __ nt ____________

4. j __ __ n ____________

5. c __ __ n ____________

6. n __ __ se ____________

7. __ __ l ____________

H. Using Other Word Forms Add an ending to each word to write an Other Word Form.

1. oil + y = ________________
2. deliver + y = ________________
3. shine + y = ________________
4. noise + y = ________________
5. slice + ing = ________________

I. Challenge Words Write the Challenge Word that completes each word pair.

elbow	**moist**	**driver**	**shivers**	**wedding**

1. knee or ________________
2. marriage or ________________
3. passenger or ________________
4. trembles or ________________
5. damp or ________________

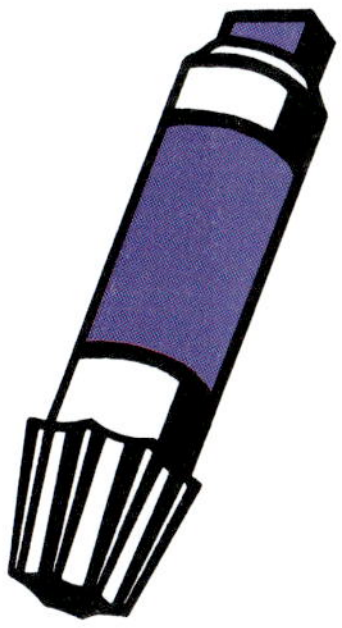

J. Spelling and Writing Write each set of words in a sentence. You may use Other Word Forms. Proofread your work.

1. river – noise
2. September – Wednesday
3. sliced – boil
4. oil – soil
5. writer – point
6. shining – coin
7. driving – deliver
8. women – join
9. sliding – silver
10. wedding – driver
11. moist – shivers
12. elbow – slid

15

A. Pretest and Proofreading

B. Spelling Words and Phrases

1.	dawn	just before dawn
2.	lawn	a lawn mower
3.	laws	passed new laws
4.	draw	had to draw straws
5.	straw	a bale of straw
6.	lean	to lean against
7.	meal	finished the meal
8.	weak	a weak voice
9.	fears	often fears danger
10.	earn	whatever we earn
11.	early	early the next day
12.	earth	the rotation of the earth
13.	heard	heard an echo
14.	heart	a valentine heart
15.	hammer	a hammer and a nail
16.	matter	doesn't matter
17.	madder	madder than ever
18.	ladder	up the ladder

Other Word Forms

dawns, dawned, dawning
lawns
law, lawful, lawyer
draws, drew, drawing
drawer
straws
leans, leaned, leaning
meals
weaker, weakest, weakly
fear, feared, fearing,
fearful
earns, earned, earning
earlier, earliest
earthy, earthly
hear, hears, hearing
hearts, hearty,
heartier, heartiest
hammers, hammered,
hammering
matters
mad, maddest, madly
ladders

C. Visual Warm-up Write each word in its correct shape.

a. b. c. d. e. f. g. h. i. j. k. l. m. n. o. p. q. r.

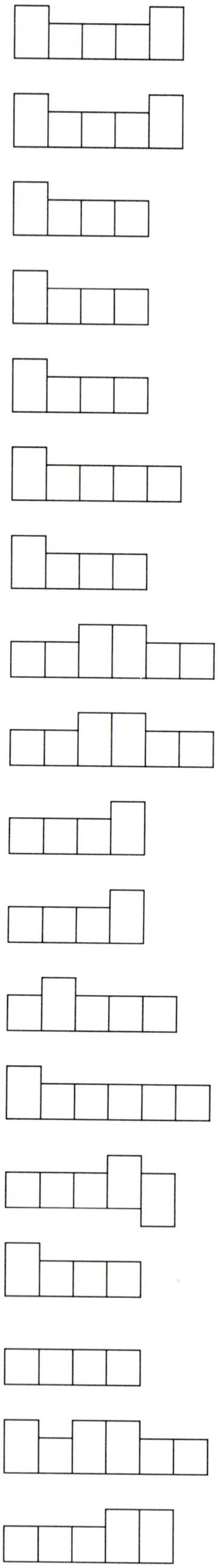

D. Missing Vowels Find the missing vowels and write the spelling words.

1. l ___ ___ n ______________
2. ___ ___ rl ___ ______________
3. d ___ wn ______________
4. h ___ mm ___ r ______________
5. l ___ dd ___ r ______________
6. dr ___ w ______________
7. m ___ dd ___ r ______________
8. m ___ tt ___ r ______________
9. h ___ ___ rd ______________
10. l ___ wn ______________
11. ___ ___ rn ______________
12. h ___ ___ rt ______________
13. str ___ w ______________
14. ___ ___ rth ______________
15. m ___ ___ l ______________
16. l ___ ws ______________
17. w ___ ___ k ______________
18. f ___ ___ rs ______________

E. Base Words The spelling list contains fourteen base words and four words that are not base words. Write each spelling word.

	Words That Are Not Base Words	Base Words
1.	earning	______________
2.	earliest	______________
3.	meals	______________
4.	matters	______________
5.	dawning	______________
6.	ladders	______________
7.	weakly	______________
8.	hammering	______________
9.	lawns	______________
10.	heartiest	______________
11.	straws	______________
12.	leaning	______________
13.	drew	______________
14.	earthly	______________
15.	______________	hear
16.	______________	mad
17.	______________	fear
18.	______________	law

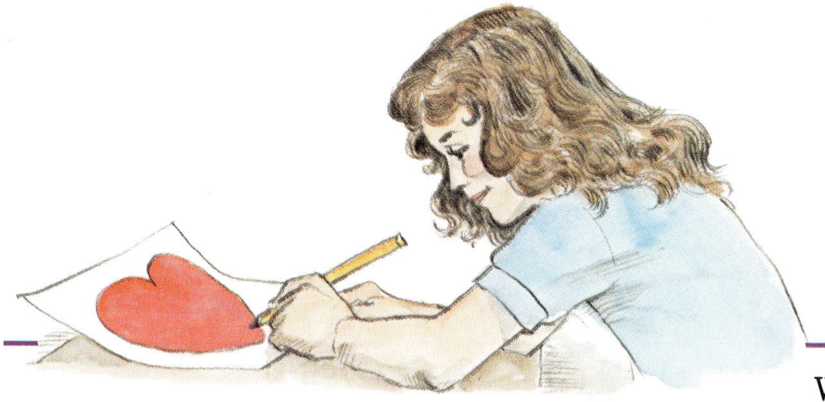

Spelling Words

dawn	lawn	laws	draw	straw	lean
meal	weak	fears	earn	early	earth
heard	heart	hammer	matter	madder	ladder

F. Rearrange and Change How fast can you rearrange the scrambled words to make all of the spelling words? Ask a partner to time you. You must write each word. Ready? Begin!

1.	2.	3.	4.	5.	6.
wnad	wadr	wastr	rthae	ealm	neal
7.	**8.**	**9.**	**10.**	**11.**	**12.**
redlad	arne	yearl	searf	keaw	awls
13.	**14.**	**15.**	**16.**	**17.**	**18.**
remham	tremat	harde	awnl	dremad	thear

Spelling Words

1. ____________	7. ____________	13. ____________
2. ____________	8. ____________	14. ____________
3. ____________	9. ____________	15. ____________
4. ____________	10. ____________	16. ____________
5. ____________	11. ____________	17. ____________
6. ____________	12. ____________	18. ____________

Record your time.

Minutes ____________ Seconds ____________

G. Using Other Word Forms Write the Other Word Form that fits each series.

Base Words: fear(ing) hammer(ing) weak(est) hearty(est) draw(ing)

1. draws, drew, ____________________
2. fears, feared, ____________________
3. hammers, hammered, ____________________
4. weak, weaker, ____________________
5. hearty, heartier, ____________________

H. Challenge Words Write the Challenge Word that completes each phrase.

earlier	**balcony**	**salad**	**shawl**	**seize**

1. either a porch or a ____________________
2. either a scarf or a ____________________
3. either sooner or ____________________
4. either vegetables or a ____________________
5. either grab or ____________________

I. Spelling and Writing Read the story idea. Use the Spelling Words, Other Word Forms, and Challenge Words to help you think of an answer to each question. Proofread your work.

Story idea:
The loud hammering woke us from a sound sleep.

1. Who heard the loud hammering?
2. How did the characters feel about being woken up?
3. How did the characters feel about the noise?
4. Who or what made the hammering noise?
5. Where did this happen?
6. What time of day was it?

16

A. Pretest and Proofreading

B. Spelling Words and Phrases

1.	death	sudden death
2.	breath	out of breath
3.	ahead	far ahead
4.	thread	needle and thread
5.	already	already there
6.	wear	will wear a coat
7.	lightly	stepped lightly
8.	lightning	flash of lightning
9.	broke	broke in two
10.	globe	the spinning globe
11.	froze	froze solid
12.	November	the end of November
13.	score	the winning score
14.	porch	under the porch
15.	Tuesday	Tuesday afternoon
16.	music	distant music
17.	few	a few children
18.	during	during the morning

Other Word Forms

deaths, deathly
breaths, breathed, breathing, breathless
threads, threading
wears, wore, worn, wearing
light, lights, lit, lighting, lighter, lightest
break, breaks, breaking, broken
globes, global
freeze, freezes, frozen, freezing
Nov.
scores, scoring
porches
Tues.
musical, musically, musician
fewer, fewest

C. Visual Warm-up

Write each word in its correct shape.

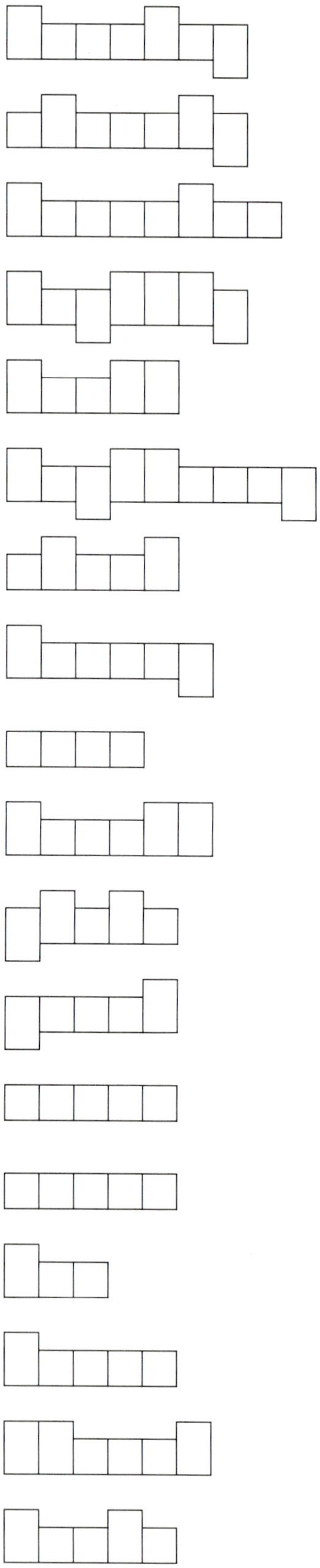

a. b. c. d. e. f. g. h. i. j. k. l. m. n. o. p. q. r.

D. Word Match-ups Find a word in the spelling list that best fits each word or phrase below. Write each word. Check your answers in the **Spelling Dictionary**.

1. in front ____________
2. the total of points in a game ____________
3. a model of the earth ____________
4. an autumn month ____________
5. thin string ____________
6. to have clothing on ____________
7. screened-in room ____________
8. notes and scales ____________
9. a weekday ____________
10. made cold and solid ____________
11. at some point of time ____________
12. not many ____________
13. goes with thunder ____________
14. air taken into the body ____________
15. came apart ____________
16. softly ____________
17. the end of life ____________
18. by this time ____________

E. Word Clues Be a detective. Study the clues to uncover the words from the spelling list. Write the words.

1. clef, note, staff, conductor, ____________
2. dark, stormy, thunder, flash, ____________
3. Thanksgiving, cold, football, month, ____________
4. weekday, school, work, study, ____________
5. chairs, front, house, outside, ____________
6. team, goal, points, touchdown, ____________
7. earth, round, equator, axis, ____________
8. tailor, sew, needle, stitch, ____________
9. gasp, inhale, air, oxygen, ____________

Spelling Words

death	breath	ahead	thread	already
wear	lightly	lightning	broke	globe
froze	November	score	porch	Tuesday
music	few	during		

F. Guide Words These word pairs are guide words that might appear in a dictionary. Write the words from the spelling list that would appear on the same page as each pair of guide words.

Example:

huge – kept

hunter

iron

above – ax

1. ______
2. ______

blame – bucket

3. ______
4. ______

correct – dirt

5. ______

dirty – evening

6. ______

event – flock

7. ______

floor – gang

8. ______

get – hate

9. ______

leaf – lucky

10. ______
11. ______

mean – nineteen

12. ______

nobody – outfit

13. ______

pocket – purse

14. ______

scale – sheet

15. ______

stream – thread

16. ______

throw – unlock

17. ______

until – worry

18. ______

G. Using Other Word Forms Write the Other Word Form that fits each clue.

Base Words: break(ing) breath(less) score(ing) light(ing) globe(al)

1. short of breath ________________
2. making points in a game ________________
3. all over the world ________________
4. destroying ________________
5. adding light to an area ________________

H. Challenge Words Write the Challenge Word that completes each question.

beauty	**duty**	**fuel**	**insure**	**stored**

1. What type of ________________ is used to heat the house?
2. Where is the furniture ________________?
3. Is there ________________ in a sunset?
4. Should I ________________ my car against collision damage?
5. Who has a ________________ to perform?

I. Spelling and Writing Write each set of words in a sentence. You may use Other Word Forms. Proofread your work.

1. lightly – music
2. few – breath
3. wear – froze
4. lightning – ahead
5. score – during
6. Tuesday – November
7. broke – globe
8. porch – thread
9. already – death
10. duty – insure
11. fuel – stored
12. beauty – breathless

17

A. Pretest and Proofreading

B. Spelling Words and Phrases

1.	**until**	until you come
2.	**study**	tried to study
3.	**lucky**	your lucky charm
4.	**bucket**	the bucket of cement
5.	**number**	remembered their number
6.	**Sunday**	Sunday gathering
7.	**sir**	sir or madam
8.	**shirt**	checkered shirt
9.	**dirty**	dirty clothes
10.	**birthday**	my next birthday
11.	**leaf**	a yellow leaf
12.	**leak**	a leak in the hose
13.	**leading**	leading the race
14.	**heating**	heating the water
15.	**scold**	to scold for nothing
16.	**oldest**	oldest in the family
17.	**holding**	holding tighter
18.	**poster**	baseball poster

Other Word Forms

studies, studied, studying, student, studious
luckier, luckiest, luckily
buckets
numbers, numbered, numbering
Sun.
sirs
shirts
dirtier, dirtiest
birthdays
leaves, leafy
leaks, leaked, leaking, leaky
lead, leads, led
heat, heats, heated, heater
scolds, scolded, scolding
old, older
hold, holds, held
posters

C. Visual Warm-up

Write each word in its correct shape.

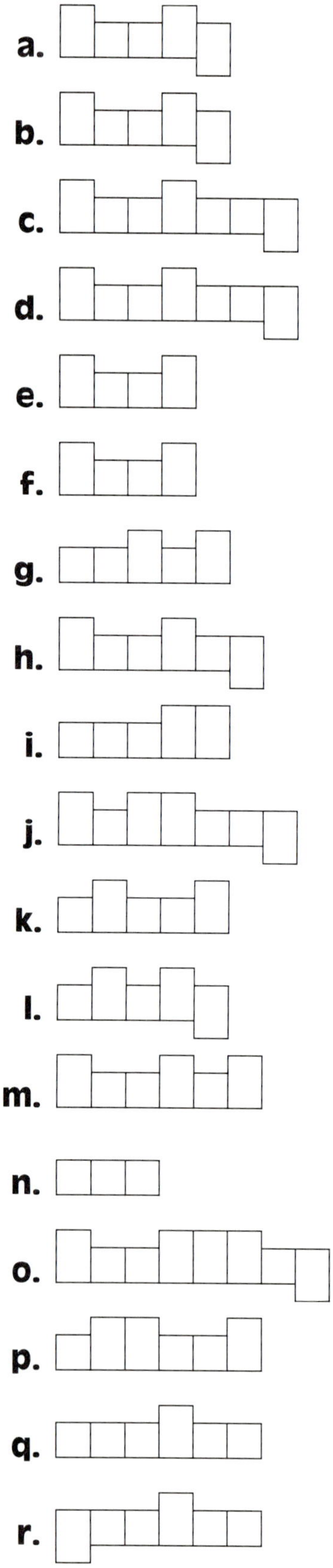

D. Sort Your Words Write each of the spelling words where it belongs.

One-syllable Words	Two-syllable Words	
1. ______	6. ______	13. ______
2. ______	7. ______	14. ______
3. ______	8. ______	15. ______
4. ______	9. ______	16. ______
5. ______	10. ______	17. ______
	11. ______	18. ______
	12. ______	

19. By adding endings to the spelling words, make four three-syllable Other Word Forms.

______ ______

______ ______

E. Break the Code Use the code to write the spelling words.

1	2	3	4	5	6	7	8	9	10	11	12	13	14	15	16	17	18	19	20
↓	↓	↓	↓	↓	↓	↓	↓	↓	↓	↓	↓	↓	↓	↓	↓	↓	↓	↓	↓
a	b	c	d	e	f	g	h	i	k	l	m	n	o	p	r	s	t	u	y

1. 11, 5, 1, 6 ______

2. 17, 8, 9, 16, 18 ______

3. 4, 9, 16, 18, 20 ______

4. 17, 18, 19, 4, 20 ______

5. 19, 13, 18, 9, 11 ______

6. 17, 3, 14, 11, 4 ______

7. 11, 5, 1, 10 ______

8. 14, 11, 4, 5, 17, 18 ______

9. 17, 9, 16 ______

10. 8, 14, 11, 4, 9, 13, 7 ______

11. 17, 19, 13, 4, 1, 20 ______

12. 15, 14, 17, 18, 5, 16 ______

13. 2, 19, 3, 10, 5, 18 ______

14. 13, 19, 12, 2, 5, 16 ______

15. 11, 19, 3, 10, 20 ______

16. 8, 5, 1, 18, 9, 13, 7 ______

17. 11, 5, 1, 4, 9, 13, 7 ______

18. 2, 9, 16, 18, 8, 4, 1, 20 ______

Spelling Words

until	study	lucky	bucket	number
Sunday	sir	shirt	dirty	birthday
leaf	leak	leading	heating	scold
oldest	holding	poster		

F. Words and Meanings Write a spelling word for each meaning. Check your answers in the **Spelling Dictionary**.

1. a day of the week ________________
2. a thin, flat part of a plant ________________
3. up to the time of ________________
4. a round container for carrying things ________________
5. to try to learn ________________
6. a hole that lets something in or out by accident ________________
7. making warm ________________
8. having lived for the longest time ________________
9. being ahead of ________________
10. a piece of clothing for the upper body ________________
11. the day on which someone is born ________________
12. a large printed notice ________________
13. a numeral connected with a person or thing ________________
14. taking and keeping in one's hands ________________
15. to blame angrily ________________
16. having good fortune ________________
17. unclean ________________
18. a title used instead of a man's name ________________

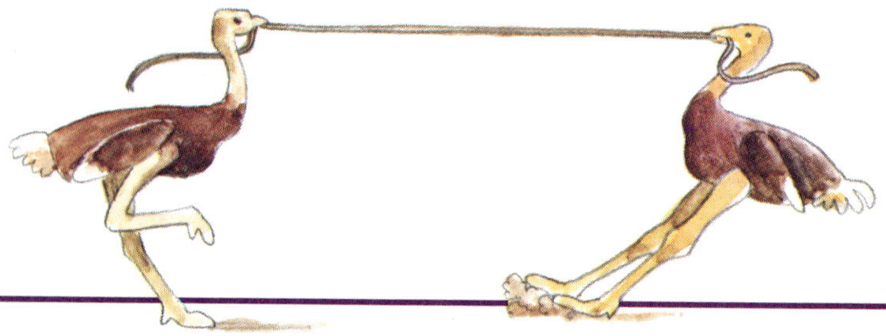

G. Using Other Word Forms Write the Other Word Form that fits each group of words.

Base Words: leak(y) study(ed) number(ed) lucky(est) leaf(es)

1. bark, trunk, roots, ____________________

2. faucet, old hose, tire losing air, ____________________

3. most fortunate, winner, ____________________

4. examined, books, test, ____________________

5. put in order, given a place, ____________________

H. Challenge Words Write the Challenge Word that completes each word pair.

ease	**folks**	**furnish**	**lumber**	**alert**

1. wide-awake and ____________________

2. wood and ____________________

3. people and ____________________

4. comfort and ____________________

5. provide and ____________________

I. Spelling and Writing Read the paragraph. Use as many Spelling Words, Other Word Forms, and Challenge Words as you can to write *two* or more answers to each question. Proofread your work.

Sometimes we think that believing in luck is an idea limited to the past. But even today many people believe that certain things can bring good fortune. Some folks think that seven is a lucky number. Others believe that birthdays or certain days of the week are especially lucky days. Some people hold onto lucky charms, such as old four-leaf clovers. Others wear clothes that they think will bring luck. Maybe just believing in luck can make good things happen.

1. What are some things that people think are lucky?

2. What are some things that people might do to bring luck?

18

REVIEWING LESSONS 13-17

■	★	▲	◆	●
mist	early	lightning	September	wear
mix	heard	Tuesday	Sunday	November
March	lightly	ahead	until	weak
Wednesday	during	already	holding	farther

A. Weather Watch Write Other Word Forms or the spelling words to complete these sentences about weather. The shapes tell you in what column you can find the spelling word. Write each word or its Other Word Form only once. If you need help, use the **Spelling Dictionary**.

1. The snowstorm came ★ _ _ _ _ _ _ _ than we expected.

2. Thunder and ▲ _ _ _ _ _ _ _ _ _ are coming our way.

3. A ■ _ _ _ _ _ fog rolled off the ocean.

4. There were a few sunny days in the month of ◆ _ _ _ _ _ _ _ _ _ .

5. You will be ● _ _ _ _ _ _ _ coats tomorrow if it gets colder.

6. For the holiday on ◆ _ _ _ _ _ _ , there will be clear skies.

7. We will be ★ _ _ _ _ _ _ _ thunder later on today.

8. The month of ● _ _ _ _ _ _ _ _ was filled with sunny days.

9. Rain ■ _ _ _ _ _ with snow is forecasted.

10. On ▲ _ _ _ _ _ _ _ there is a chance of freezing rain.

11. There will be a ★ _ _ _ _ _ snowfall tonight.

12. As the storm got closer, it got ● _ _ _ _ _ _ in strength.

13. A strong ■ _ _ _ _ _ wind will bend the trees.

14. It will be 24 hours ◆ _ _ _ _ _ the rain stops.

15. The clouds up ▲ _ _ _ _ _ look very dark.

16. The latest map shows the storm moving ● _ _ _ _ _ _ _ out to sea.

17. The storm will likely ◆ _ _ _ _ off until early evening.

18. By noon today, there ▲ _ _ _ _ _ _ _ was flooding in the streets.

19. Children missed school on ■ _ _ _ _ _ _ _ _ _ due to the hurricane.

20. Two feet of snow fell ★ _ _ _ _ _ _ the night.

REVIEW

oil	dawn	lawn	leak	draw
earn	hammer	heart	tin	few
point	join	thread	leaf	breath
deliver	lean	meal	silver	broke

B. Squaring Off Add endings to the spelling words. Write the new words in the squares. For some words you need to add or subtract a letter before adding the ending. If you need help, use the **Spelling Dictionary**.

a. Add *ing*

oil

earn

point

deliver

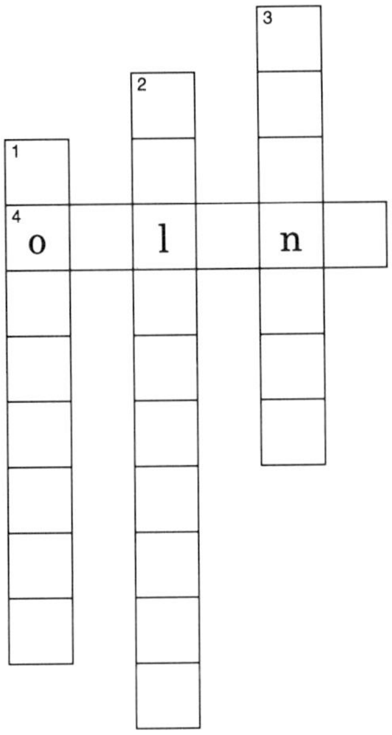

b. Add *s*

lawn

heart

thread

meal

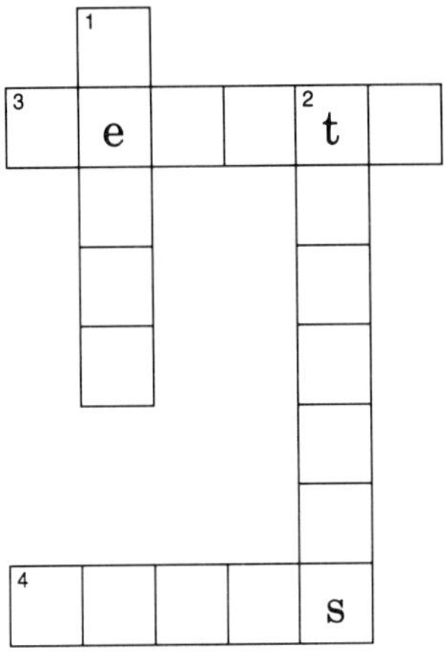

c. Add *ed*

dawn

hammer

join

lean

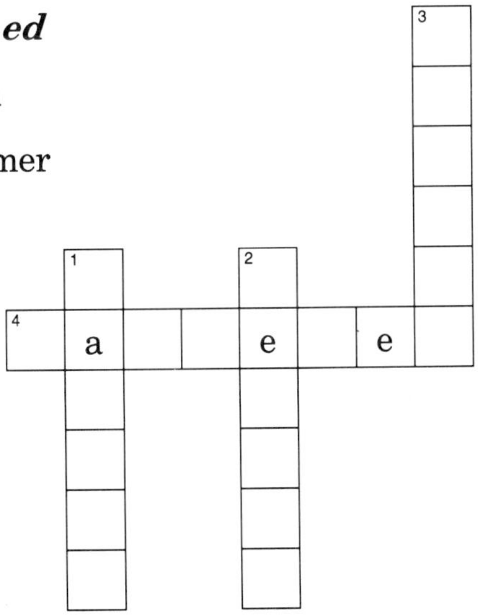

d. Add *y*

leak

tin

leaf

silver

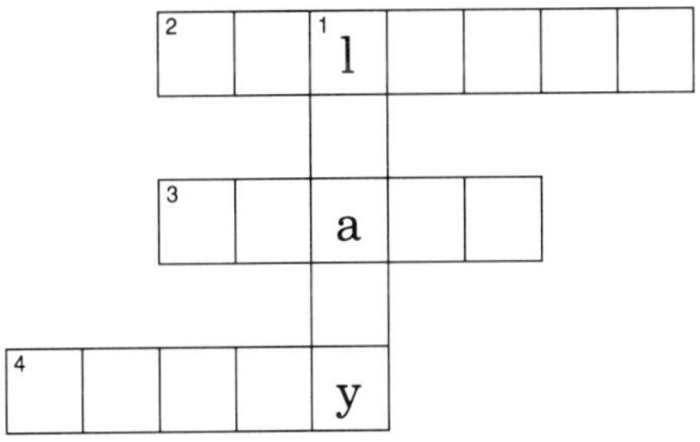

e. Add *er*

draw

few

breath

broke

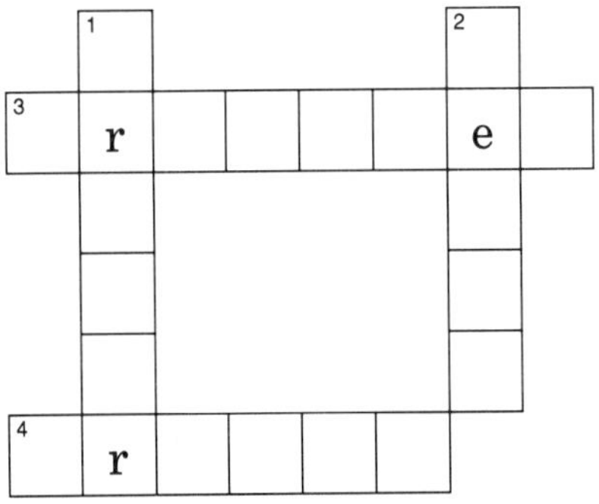

REVIEW

boil	ladder	marker	score	skating
bucket	laws	mint	shirt	sliding
earth	lucky	music	sir	straw
fears	madder	noise	sixteen	women
froze	marble	river	sixth	writer

REVIEW

C. Hidden Words Use the clues to find Other Word Forms or the spelling words in the puzzle. Circle and write each word.

b	o	i	l	i	n	g	c	m	a	r	b	l	e	s
u	p	l	a	d	d	e	r	s	s	i	w	r	m	h
c	e	o	w	s	k	a	t	e	d	v	z	d	o	i
k	m	n	a	r	j	i	m	t	v	e	b	n	s	r
e	a	r	t	h	d	b	i	u	w	r	q	p	e	t
t	o	f	e	a	r	x	n	o	r	s	i	x	c	s
s	i	x	t	e	e	n	t	h	m	a	d	n	a	m
f	r	e	e	z	e	o	m	u	s	i	c	i	a	n
b	z	y	q	u	t	i	n	o	s	l	i	d	e	s
l	u	c	k	i	e	s	t	r	a	w	y	z	w	i
s	c	o	r	e	d	e	m	a	r	k	s	t	b	r
w	r	i	t	e	x	s	w	o	m	a	n	c	t	u

Down

1. used to carry sand ___ ___ ___ ___ ___ ___ ___
2. a rule ___ ___ ___
3. unpleasant sounds ___ ___ ___ ___ ___ ___
4. a plant used for flavoring ___ ___ ___ ___
5. streams of water ___ ___ ___ ___ ___ ___
6. clothing that has sleeves ___ ___ ___ ___ ___ ___
7. a title for a man ___ ___ ___

Across

8. bubbling hot ___ ___ ___ ___ ___ ___ ___
9. polished round stones ___ ___ ___ ___ ___ ___ ___
10. used for climbing ___ ___ ___ ___ ___ ___ ___
11. moved on ice ___ ___ ___ ___ ___ ___ ___
12. our planet ___ ___ ___ ___ ___
13. to feel afraid ___ ___ ___ ___
14. after five ___ ___ ___
15. after the fifteenth ___ ___ ___ ___ ___ ___ ___ ___ ___
16. angry ___ ___ ___
17. to make water into ice ___ ___ ___ ___ ___ ___
18. violinist ___ ___ ___ ___ ___ ___ ___ ___
19. moves on a smooth surface ___ ___ ___ ___ ___ ___
20. having the best luck ___ ___ ___ ___ ___ ___ ___ ___
21. stalks of grain ___ ___ ___ ___ ___
22. made points in a game ___ ___ ___ ___ ___ ___
23. spots on a paper ___ ___ ___ ___ ___
24. to make words with a pen ___ ___ ___ ___ ___
25. an adult female ___ ___ ___ ___ ___

bid	dim	leading	porch	shining
birthday	dirty	matter	poster	sliced
chart	driving	number	replace	soil
coin	globe	oldest	reward	study
death	heating	plane	scold	ticket

D. Word Arithmetic Make one or two changes on each spelling word to write an Other Word Form.

1. replace − e + ing = ______________
2. plane + s = ______________
3. shining − ing + es = ______________
4. number + ed = ______________
5. oldest − est + er = ______________
6. bid + d + er = ______________
7. sliced − ed + ing = ______________
8. death + ly = ______________
9. study − y + ies = ______________
10. poster + s = ______________
11. reward + ed = ______________
12. soil + s = ______________
13. matter + ed = ______________
14. porch + es = ______________
15. heating − ing + ed = ______________
16. dim + ly = ______________
17. coin + ed = ______________
18. globe − e + al = ______________
19. scold + s = ______________
20. birthday + s = ______________
21. chart + ed = ______________
22. ticket + ing = ______________
23. driving − ing + es = ______________
24. leading − ing + s = ______________
25. dirty − y + ier = ______________

19

A. Pretest and Proofreading

B. Spelling Words and Phrases

1.	**iron**	to iron the clothes
2.	**island**	small island
3.	**tiny**	tiny gerbil
4.	**quiet**	quiet evening
5.	**Friday**	Friday night
6.	**provide**	will provide the meal
7.	**lamb**	heard the lamb
8.	**wrap**	to wrap the package
9.	**crack**	through the crack
10.	**crash**	will crash to the floor
11.	**flash**	done in a flash
12.	**drank**	drank too fast
13.	**blanket**	favorite blanket
14.	**glasses**	wears glasses
15.	**led**	led them away
16.	**fled**	fled from the room
17.	**shed**	hidden in the shed
18.	**monster**	my pet monster

Other Word Forms

irons, ironed, ironing
islands
tinier, tiniest
quietly, quieter, quietest
Fri.
provides, provided, providing, provider
lambs
wraps, wrapped, wrapping
cracks, cracked, cracking
crashes, crashed, crashing
flashes, flashed, flashing
drink, drinks, drinking, drunk
blankets, blanketed, blanketing
glass, glassy
lead, leads, leading
flee, flees, fleeing
sheds, shedding
monsters, monstrous

C. Visual Warm-up

Write each word in its correct shape.

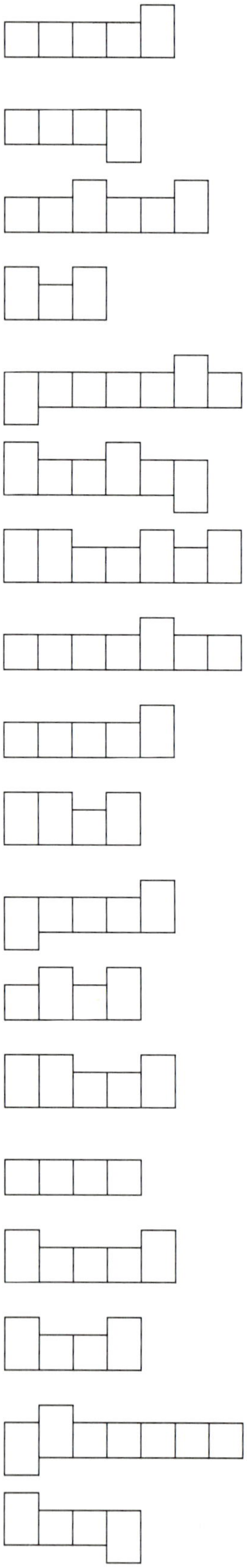

a. b. c. d. e. f. g. h. i. j. k. l. m. n. o. p. q. r.

D. Word Match-ups Find a word in the spelling list that best fits each phrase. Write each word. Check your answers in the **Spelling Dictionary**.

1. used to see better ____________
2. ran away ____________
3. land with water all around ____________
4. used on a bed to keep warm ____________
5. an ugly movie character ____________
6. unlucky day when it's 13 ____________
7. very small ____________
8. to cover with paper and tie up ____________
9. a little storage building ____________
10. opposite of *followed* ____________
11. a noisy fall ____________
12. without noise ____________
13. swallowed milk ____________
14. a long narrow opening ____________
15. a baby sheep ____________
16. a quick, bright light ____________
17. used to press clothes ____________
18. to give what is needed ____________

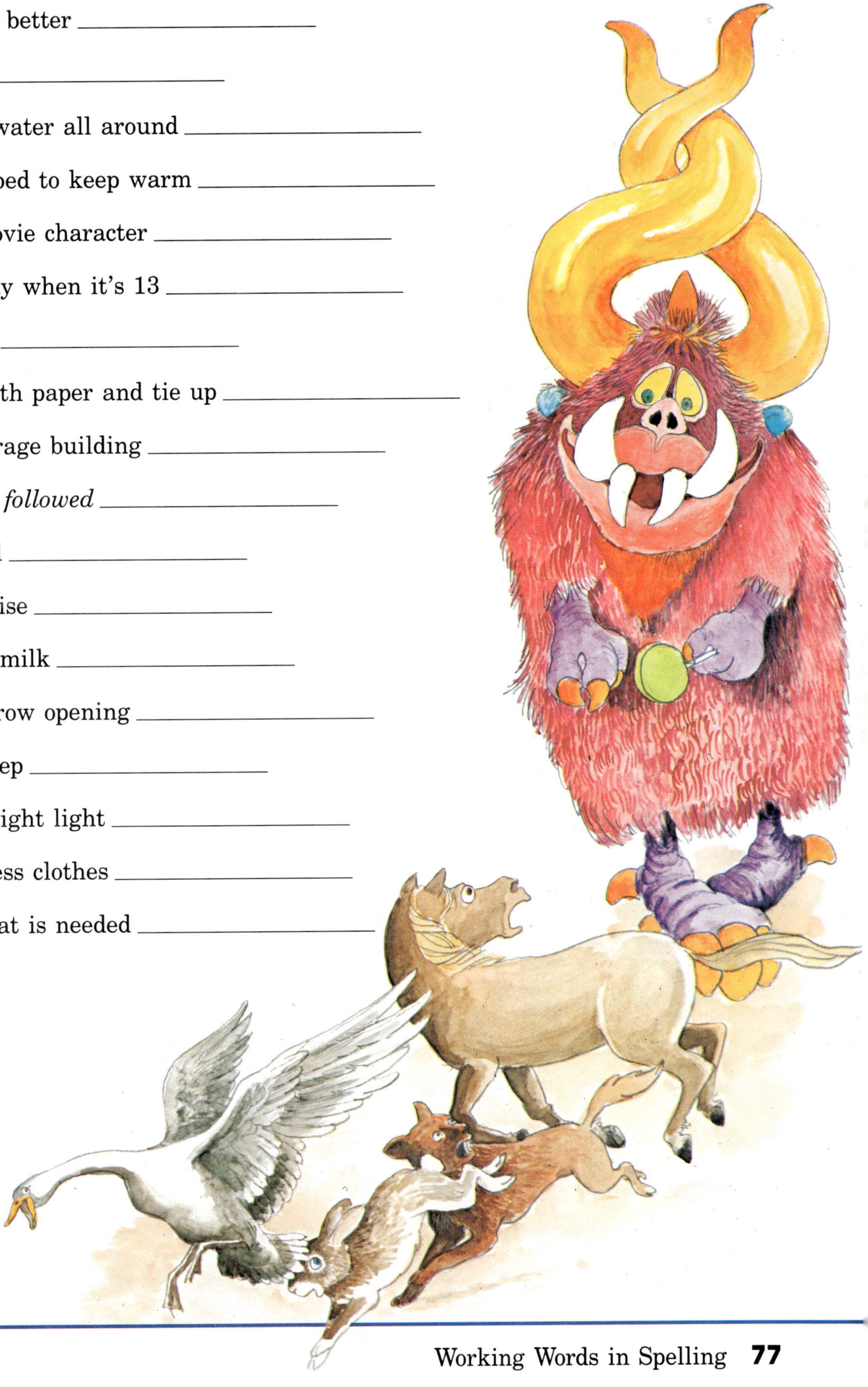

Spelling Words

iron	island	tiny	quiet	Friday	provide
lamb	wrap	crack	crash	flash	drank
blanket	glasses	led	fled	shed	monster

E. Base Words The spelling list contains fourteen base words and four words that are not base words. Write each spelling word.

	Words That Are Not Base Words	Base Words
1.	cracking	______
2.	Fri.	______
3.	blankets	______
4.	tinier	______
5.	providing	______
6.	ironing	______
7.	wrapped	______
8.	crashing	______
9.	islands	______
10.	quietly	______
11.	flashing	______
12.	monsters	______
13.	sheds	______
14.	lambs	______
15.	______	lead
16.	______	drink
17.	______	flee
18.	______	glass

F. Word Hunt The spelling words can be found in the word puzzle. The words appear across and down. Circle and write the words.

i	r	o	n	l	a	m	b	f	f
s	h	e	d	c	s	t	g	l	r
l	e	d	w	r	a	p	l	a	i
a	b	d	o	a	l	m	a	s	d
n	o	e	t	c	r	a	s	h	a
d	r	a	n	k	e	r	s	t	y
b	l	a	n	k	e	t	e	i	f
p	r	o	v	i	d	e	s	n	l
p	m	o	n	s	t	e	r	y	e
o	s	n	t	q	u	i	e	t	d

Across

1. ______
2. ______
3. ______
4. ______
5. ______
6. ______
7. ______
8. ______
9. ______
10. ______
11. ______

Down

12. ______
13. ______
14. ______
15. ______
16. ______
17. ______
18. ______

G. Using Other Word Forms

Write the Other Word Form that completes each sentence.

Base Words: monster(ous) shed(ing) flee(ing) wrap(ed) tiny(est)

1. He was running away. He was ______________ .
2. The snake was losing its skin. It was ______________ .
3. The gift was covered with paper and a bow. It was ______________ .
4. It was the smallest. It was the ______________ .
5. The plant was huge. It was ______________ .

H. Challenge Words

Write the Challenge Word that replaces each underlined word or phrase.

magnet	canned	striking	oddly	dwellings

1. Their homes are made of logs. ______________
2. The animals behaved strangely. ______________
3. The vegetables are in metal containers. ______________
4. It's a thing that attracts iron. ______________
5. What were you hitting? ______________

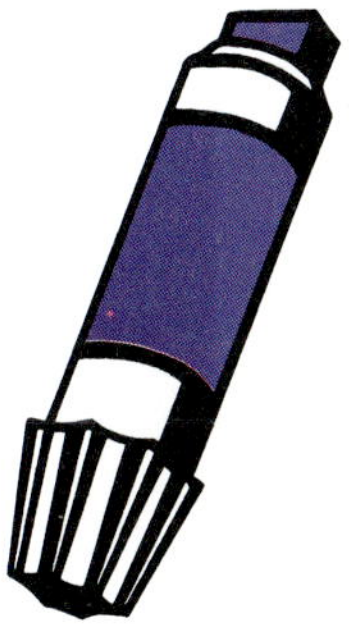

I. Spelling and Writing

Write each set of words in a sentence. You may use Other Word Forms. Proofread your work.

1. led – monster
2. wrap – shed
3. provide – lamp
4. flash – island
5. fled – crash
6. quiet – drank
7. blanket – tiny
8. crack – glasses
9. Friday – iron
10. magnet – striking
11. dwellings – canned
12. oddly – monsters

20

A. Pretest and Proofreading

B. Spelling Words and Phrases

1.	beef	all beef frankfurt
2.	heel	heel of my boot
3.	sheep	frolicking sheep
4.	steep	down the steep path
5.	agree	if you agree
6.	cheer	stood up to cheer
7.	jar	jar of cream
8.	yard	in the front yard
9.	harm	no harm done
10.	party	invited to the party
11.	partly	partly completed
12.	candle	lighted candle
13.	handle	broom handle
14.	paddle	will paddle up the stream
15.	saddle	an old western saddle
16.	banner	the school banner
17.	battle	a battle for first place
18.	cattle	cattle on the range

Other Word Forms

beefy
heels, heeled
sheepish
steeper, steepest
agrees, agreed, agreeing, agreeable
cheers, cheered, cheering, cheery, cheerful
jars, jarred, jarring
yards
harms, harmed, harming, harmful
parties, partying
part, parts, parted, parting
candles
handles, handled, handling
paddles, paddled, paddling
saddles, saddled, saddling
banners
battles, battled, battling

C. Visual Warm-up

Write each word in its correct shape.

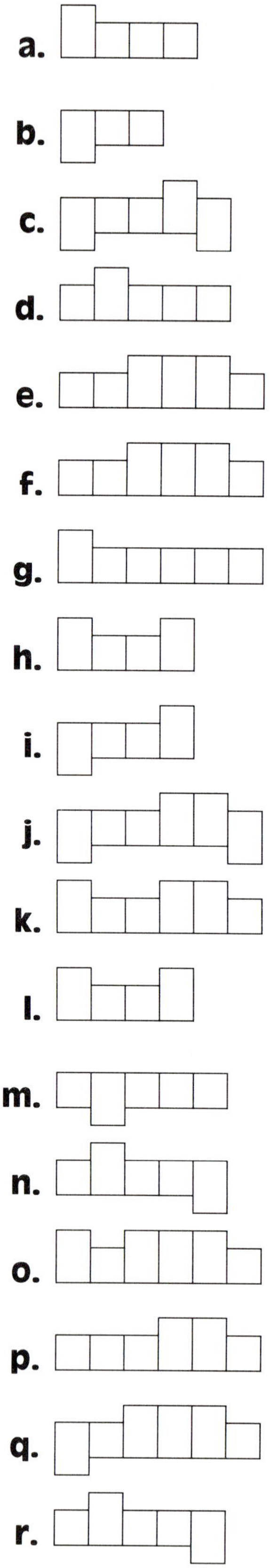

D. Words and Meanings Write a spelling word for each meaning. Check your answers in the **Spelling Dictionary**.

1. an animal with thick wool and hooves ________________
2. an area of ground around a house ________________
3. meat from cattle ________________
4. a fight ________________
5. to give a happy shout ________________
6. having an almost straight up-and-down slope ________________
7. the part of an object held by the hand ________________
8. to think the same as another ________________
9. a seat for riding on a horse ________________
10. part of a shoe ________________
11. a flag ________________
12. to move a canoe with an oar ________________
13. cows and bulls ________________
14. a glass or clay container ________________
15. in part ________________
16. a stick of wax with a wick ________________
17. people gathered to have fun ________________
18. damage or injury ________________

E. Hinky Pinky The solution to each Hinky Pinky is two rhyming words, each with two syllables. Solve each Hinky Pinky. At least one word of each Hinky Pinky will be a spelling word.

Example: This is very strong tall building. *power tower*

1. This holds something that gives light in darkness. ________________
2. Two cows' fighting is called this. ________________
3. This is an event for bright people. ________________
4. A riding cowboy uses this to budge his horse. ________________
5. This is a person who plans a pattern for a flag. ________________

Spelling Words

beef	heel	sheep	steep	agree	cheer
jar	yard	harm	party	partly	candle
handle	paddle	saddle	banner	battle	cattle

F. Sort Your Words In alphabetical order, write the spelling words where they belong.

Words with an *ar*	Words with Two *e*'s	Words with an *le* Ending
1. ______	6. ______	12. ______
2. ______	7. ______	13. ______
3. ______	8. ______	14. ______
4. ______	9. ______	15. ______
5. ______	10. ______	16. ______
	11. ______	17. ______

18. Write the one word not used above. ______

G. Break the Code Use the code to write the spelling words.

a	b	c	d	e	f	g	h	i	j	k	l	m
↕	↕	↕	↕	↕	↕	↕	↕	↕	↕	↕	↕	↕
z	y	x	w	v	u	t	s	r	q	p	o	n

1. xzmwov ______

2. kzwwov ______

3. qzi ______

4. xzggov ______

5. szin ______

6. ztivv ______

7. svvo ______

8. yzmmvi ______

9. kzigb ______

10. xsvvi ______

11. hzwwov ______

12. kzigob ______

13. yzggov ______

14. hsvvk ______

15. hgvvk ______

16. szmwov ______

17. bziw ______

18. yvvu ______

H. Using Other Word Forms

Write the Other Word Form that fits each series.

Base Words: handle(ing) saddle(ing) battle(ing) jar(ed) paddle(ing)

1. jars, ______________, jarring
2. paddles, paddled, ______________
3. saddles, saddled, ______________
4. battles, battled, ______________
5. handles, handled, ______________

I. Challenge Words

Write the Challenge Word that completes each phrase.

nearly	**rattlesnake**	**scarlet**	**harmless**	**zebra**

1. either red or ______________
2. either almost or ______________
3. either a cobra or a ______________
4. either a horse or a ______________
5. either safe or ______________

J. Spelling and Writing

Read the story idea. Use the Spelling Words, Other Word Forms, and Challenge Words to help you think of an answer to each question. Proofread your work.

Story idea:
Thousands of frightened cattle stampeded through the gates.

1. Where were the cattle?
2. Why were they frightened?
3. What damage did the cattle cause?
4. Where did the cattle end up?
5. Who saw the cattle running?
6. What did the character(s) do about this situation?

21

A. Pretest and Proofreading

B. Spelling Words and Phrases

1.	ton	a ton of coal
2.	job	another job
3.	sob	a frightened sob
4.	fond	fond of swimming
5.	chop	a thick lamb chop
6.	copy	will copy over again
7.	bother	doesn't bother me
8.	wrong	wrong time
9.	strong	strong harness
10.	belonged	belonged together
11.	burn	if it will burn
12.	nurse	the night nurse
13.	purse	found my purse
14.	turtle	the sunning turtle
15.	returning	returning the books
16.	sure	is sure of the answer
17.	grind	to grind the grain
18.	remind	if you remind me

Other Word Forms

tons
jobs
sobs, sobbed, sobbing
fonder, fondest, fondly
chops, chopped, chopping
copies, copied, copying
bothers, bothered, bothering
wronged, wrongly
strongly, stronger, strongest
belong, belongs, belonging, belongings
burns, burned, burning, burner
nurses, nursed, nursing
purses
turtles
return, returns, returned
surest, surely
grinds, ground, grinding, grinder
reminds, reminded, reminding

C. Visual Warm-up

Write each word in its correct shape.

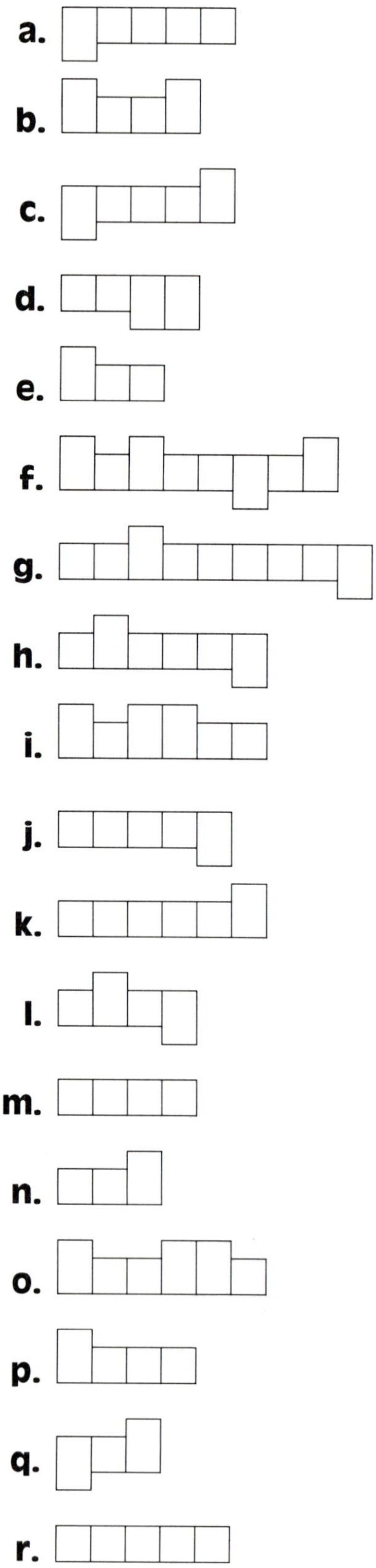

D. Bases and Suffixes The spelling list contains sixteen base words and two words with suffixes. Write each spelling word.

Words with Suffixes	Base Words	Words with Suffixes	Base Words
1. tons	________	**10.** sobbing	________
2. nursing	________	**11.** bothering	________
3. jobs	________	**12.** reminding	________
4. chopping	________	**13.** fondest	________
5. copies	________	**14.** grinding	________
6. surest	________	**15.** burner	________
7. purses	________	**16.** wrongly	________
8. turtles	________	**17.** ________	belong
9. strongest	________	**18.** ________	return

E. Guide Words These word pairs are guide words that might appear in a dictionary. Write the words from the spelling list that would appear on the same page as each pair of guide words.

backward – bucket

1. ________

2. ________

build – change

3. ________

chart – corner

4. ________

5. ________

floor – gang

6. ________

get – kept

7. ________

8. ________

nobody – outfit

9. ________

pocket – purse

10. ________

queen – return

11. ________

returning – saves

12. ________

sob – thread

13. ________

14. ________

15. ________

throw – unlock

16. ________

17. ________

worth – yellow

18. ________

Spelling Words

ton job sob fond chop
copy bother wrong strong belonged
burn nurse purse turtle returning
sure grind remind

F. Crossword Puzzle Solve the puzzle by using words from the spelling list. Write the words. Check your answers in the **Spelling Dictionary**.

Across

1. to trouble or pester
4. was a member of
5. 2,000 pounds
6. to cut with a sharp tool
7. the opposite of *right*
8. a hospital worker
9. a container for money
11. certain
13. to make into powder
14. work that has to be done
15. loving or liking

Down

1. pain from a fire
2. coming back
3. to make someone remember
5. a slow animal
6. one of many of the same
10. not weak
12. to cry

G. Using Other Word Forms Write the Other Word Form that completes each sentence.

Base Words: fond(ly) copy(ed) remind(ing) chop(ing) sob(ing)

1. The child was ________________ after the fall.
2. I am always ________________ myself to do things.
3. The cook was ________________ the vegetables.
4. The student ________________ the word incorrectly.
5. The doe looked ________________ at her fawn.

H. Challenge Words Write the Challenge Word that fits each clue.

coffee	turf	bothered	title	turkey

1. the name of a book ________________
2. a Thanksgiving treat ________________
3. a flavor of ice cream ________________
4. the surface layer of grass ________________
5. annoyed or irritated ________________

I. Spelling and Writing Write each set of words in a sentence. You may use Other Word Forms. Proofread your work.

1. nurse – burn
2. sob – purse
3. strong – ton
4. fond – belonged
5. copy – bother
6. sure – remind
7. turtle – returning
8. grind – chop
9. wrong – job
10. coffee – bothered
11. turkey – turf
12. title – copied

22

A. Pretest and Proofreading

B. Spelling Words and Phrases

1.	real	the real thing
2.	seat	on the back seat
3.	team	the winning team
4.	tear	tear in my eye
5.	feeling	feeling better
6.	meeting	attended the meeting
7.	weekend	next weekend
8.	between	between two slices of bread
9.	coal	lump of hard coal
10.	coach	the football coach
11.	chose	chose a partner
12.	phone	answered the phone
13.	stole	if they stole it
14.	smoke	smell of smoke
15.	spoke	spoke harshly
16.	sport	my favorite sport
17.	shore	drifted into shore
18.	stories	has read more stories

Other Word Forms

really
seats, seated, seating
teams
tears, teared, tearing, tearful
feel, feels, felt
meet, meets, met
weekends
coals
coaches, coached, coaching
choose, chooses, chosen, choosing
phones, phoned, phoning
steal, steals, stealing, stolen
smokes, smoked, smoking, smoky
speak, speaks, spoken, speaking, speaker
sports
shores
story

C. Visual Warm-up
Write each word in its correct shape.

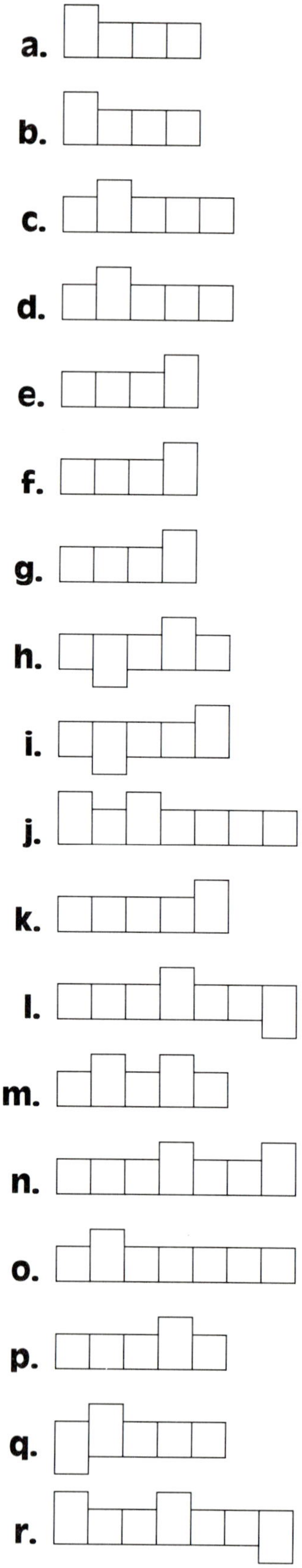

D. All in a Row Write the eighteen spelling words in alphabetical order. Then join the boxed letters and write four hidden words.

1. _ _ _ ☐ _ _ _
2. _ ☐ _ _ _
3. _ _ ☐ _ _
4. _ _ _ ☐
5. _ _ ☐ _ _ _ _
6. Hidden Word: ________________
7. ☐ _ _ _ _ _ _
8. _ _ _ _ ☐
9. _ _ ☐ _
10. _ _ _ ☐
11. Hidden Word: ________________
12. _ ☐ _ _ _
13. _ _ ☐ _ _
14. _ _ ☐ _ _
15. _ ☐ _ _ _
16. ☐ _ _ _ _
17. Hidden Word: ________________
18. ☐ _ _ _ _ _ _
19. _ ☐ _ _
20. _ ☐ _ _
21. _ _ _ _ _ _ ☐
22. Hidden Word: ________________

E. Base Words The spelling list contains twelve base words and six words that are not base words. Write each spelling word.

	Words That Are Not Base Words	Base Words		Words That Are Not Base Words	Base Words
1.	teams	________	10.	coaches	________
2.	sports	________	11.	tearing	________
3.	seating	________	12.	________	feel
4.	shores	________	13.	________	meet
5.	really	________	14.	________	story
6.	smoking	________	15.	________	steal
7.	coals	________	16.	________	choose
8.	phoned	________	17.	________	speak
9.	weekends	________			

18. Write the one base word not used above. ________________

Spelling Words

real	seat	team	tear	feeling	meeting
weekend	between	coal	coach	chose	phone
stole	smoke	spoke	sport	shore	stories

F. Out of Order The underlined word in each sentence does not make sense because the letters in it are out of order. Rearrange the letters so the sentence makes sense. Write the word change.

1. The stea must be painted again. ____________
2. Children enjoy rosties and fairy tales. ____________
3. Baseball is a popular rtosp. ____________
4. The eamt had a winning season. ____________
5. A eart ran down my face. ____________
6. Is that jewel fake or aler? ____________
7. Clams are found near the reosh. ____________
8. He keosp about your problem. ____________
9. Who secho the winner? ____________
10. I will rake the leaves this ndekewe. ____________
11. Who is the team's choac? ____________
12. Why are you englife sad? ____________
13. The thief lesto my car. ____________
14. The nepho did not ring. ____________
15. She wrote tweeben the lines. ____________
16. The engtime will come to order. ____________
17. Thick kesmo rose from the chimney. ____________
18. You can burn laco in this stove. ____________

G. Using Other Word Forms Write the Other Word Form that is the opposite of each word.

Base Words: tear(ful) real(ly) choose(ing) speak(er) coach(es)

1. players ____________________
2. assigning ____________________
3. joyful ____________________
4. listener ____________________
5. not actually ____________________

H. Challenge Words Write the Challenge Word that completes each group of words.

roasting	codes	hoarse	fleeing	series

1. signals, dots and dashes, secret, ____________________
2. husky voice, sore throat, ____________________
3. cooking, baking, oven, ____________________
4. escaping, running away, ____________________
5. set, group of stories, television, ____________________

I. Spelling and Writing Write *two* or more answers to each question. Use as many Spelling Words, Other Word Forms, and Challenge Words as you can. A few words are suggested. Proofread your work.

1. What might happen if you were cooking a meal on the grill and you burned everything?

   feeling – hoarse – smoke – coal – roasting

2. What would you do if you were leading a big race and someone passed you just before you crossed the finish line?

   meeting – weekend – team – sport – coach

3. What would you say to the principal if you couldn't find your bicycle in the schoolyard?

   stole – phone – codes – spoke – fleeing

23

A. Pretest and Proofreading

B. Spelling Words and Phrases

1.	alone	was never alone
2.	awoke	awoke early
3.	glow	the glow of the fire
4.	golden	golden sunset
5.	rolled	rolled across the floor
6.	hoping	hoping to go
7.	nobody	but nobody called
8.	greet	will greet them at the door
9.	teeth	brushed my teeth
10.	indeed	was indeed welcome
11.	event	next event
12.	level	made it level
13.	clever	clever stunt
14.	eleven	eleven and one
15.	seventh	the seventh child
16.	laugh	had to laugh
17.	January	a January storm
18.	Saturday	going away Saturday

Other Word Forms

awake, awakes, awaking, awoken
glows, glowed, glowing
gold
roll, rolls, rolling, roller
hope, hopes, hoped, hopeful, hopefully
greets, greeted, greeting
tooth, toothy
events, eventful
levels, leveled, leveling
cleverer, cleverest
eleventh
seven
laughs, laughed, laughing, laughable
Jan.
Sat.

C. Visual Warm-up

Write each word in its correct shape.

a.

b.

c.

d.

e.

f.

g.

h.

i.

j.

k.

l.

m.

n.

o.

p.

q.

r.

D. Find the Missing Treasure Unscramble the letters in the footprints and discover all the spelling words. Write the words.

1. vercle
2. pihong
3. theet
4. aaurnyJ
5. ghaul
6. vente
7. yoodnb
8. veeenl
9. wogl
10. doller
11. veell
12. nthseev
13. egret
14. naloe
15. koaew
16. durtaayS
17. deined
18. neldog

1. ________	7. ________	13. ________
2. ________	8. ________	14. ________
3. ________	9. ________	15. ________
4. ________	10. ________	16. ________
5. ________	11. ________	17. ________
6. ________	12. ________	18. ________

E. Word Search The spelling words can be found in the puzzle. The words appear across and down. Circle and write the words.

a	s	a	t	u	r	d	a	y	t	t	i
w	g	l	o	w	o	g	r	e	e	t	n
o	n	w	v	o	l	a	u	g	h	l	d
k	c	l	e	v	e	r	t	o	o	b	e
e	l	e	v	e	n	x	n	l	p	n	e
a	s	v	e	e	c	d	o	d	i	o	d
l	i	e	n	z	y	c	d	e	n	b	o
o	l	l	t	e	e	t	h	n	g	o	f
n	r	o	l	l	e	d	f	x	u	d	n
e	o	p	r	j	a	n	u	a	r	y	s
t	o	s	e	v	e	n	t	h	o	p	o

Across

1. ________
2. ________
3. ________
4. ________
5. ________
6. ________
7. ________
8. ________
9. ________
10. ________

Down

11. ________
12. ________
13. ________
14. ________
15. ________
16. ________
17. ________
18. ________

Spelling Words

alone	awoke	glow	golden	rolled
hoping	nobody	greet	teeth	indeed
event	level	clever	eleven	seventh
laugh	January	Saturday		

F. Words and Meanings Write a spelling word for each meaning. Check your answers in the **Spelling Dictionary**.

1. bright-yellow ________________
2. turned over and over ________________
3. by oneself ________________
4. no person ________________
5. to welcome in a friendly way ________________
6. light made by a fire ________________
7. to make sounds that show happiness ________________
8. woke up ________________
9. really ________________
10. a day of the week ________________
11. skillful ________________
12. the first month in the year ________________
13. wishing ________________
14. after the sixth ________________
15. one more than ten ________________
16. more than one tooth ________________
17. at an equal height ________________
18. a contest in a sports program ________________

G. Using Other Word Forms Write the Other Word Form that completes each phrase.

Base Words: hope(ful) level(ing) awake(ing) event(ful) laugh(ing)

1. not boring, but ________________
2. not hopeless, but ________________
3. not making uneven, but ________________
4. not crying, but ________________
5. not falling asleep, but ________________

H. Challenge Words Write the Challenge Word that fits each question.

crackers	theme	greeting	eleventh	spoken

1. Are oral stories always ________________ ?
2. Who's the ________________ member of the football team?
3. Who is ________________ the guests?
4. What is the ________________ of your story?
5. Do you like ________________ with peanut butter?

I. Spelling and Writing Write each set of words in a sentence. You may use Other Word Forms. Proofread your work.

1. laugh – rolled
2. glow – golden
3. nobody – clever
4. indeed – alone
5. event – level
6. hoping – seventh
7. greet – eleven
8. January – awoke
9. teeth – Saturday
10. spoken – greeting
11. eleventh – crackers
12. theme – laughed

24

REVIEWING LESSONS 19-23

■	★	▲	◆	●
iron	January	island	blanket	sheep
nurse	banner	party	candle	weekend
team	coach	event	flash	stories
phone	shed	Friday	purse	teeth

A. What's the Name Write Other Word Forms or the spelling words to name the items below. The shapes tell you in what column you can find the spelling word. Write each word or its Other Word Form only once. If you need help, use the **Spelling Dictionary**.

1. You use these to keep warm on cold nights. ◆ ___ ___ ___ ___ ___ ___ ___ ___
2. This month begins a new year. ★ ___ ___ ___ ___ ___ ___ ___
3. These animals grow thick wool. ● ___ ___ ___ ___ ___
4. These are heated and used to press clothing. ■ ___ ___ ___ ___ ___
5. These lands are surrounded by water. ▲ ___ ___ ___ ___ ___ ___ ___
6. They light up a birthday cake. ◆ ___ ___ ___ ___ ___ ___ ___
7. You buy these flags at baseball games. ★ ___ ___ ___ ___ ___ ___ ___
8. They care for sick people. ■ ___ ___ ___ ___ ___ ___
9. This is the end of every week. ● ___ ___ ___ ___ ___ ___ ___
10. You form these to play football. ■ ___ ___ ___ ___ ___
11. These are held on birthdays. ▲ ___ ___ ___ ___ ___ ___ ___
12. You see these bright lights after thunder. ◆ ___ ___ ___ ___ ___ ___ ___ of lightning
13. They teach people on sports teams. ★ ___ ___ ___ ___ ___ ___ ___
14. You read this in a book. ● ___ ___ ___ ___ ___
15. These are big happenings. ▲ ___ ___ ___ ___ ___ ___
16. You use this to talk to someone. ■ ___ ___ ___ ___ ___
17. People store garden tools in these. ★ ___ ___ ___ ___ ___
18. It comes after Thursday. ▲ ___ ___ ___ ___ ___ ___
19. People use these to hold items. ◆ ___ ___ ___ ___ ___ ___
20. You use these to chew food. ● ___ ___ ___ ___ ___

REVIEW

wrap	feeling	crash	glasses	partly
level	meeting	agree	bother	belonged
returning	burn	rolled	greet	glow
hoping	laugh	sport	copy	grind

B. Bases and Endings

Write an Other Word Form for each base word. If you need help, use the **Spelling Dictionary**.

1. wrap
2. level
3. burn
4. laugh
5. crash
6. agree
7. sport
8. bother
9. greet
10. copy
11. glow
12. grind

Write the base word and one Other Word Form for each spelling word. If you need help, use the **Spelling Dictionary**.

Spelling Word	Base Word	Other Word Form
Example: returning	*r e t u r n*	*returned*
13. hoping		
14. feeling		
15. meeting		
16. rolled		
17. glasses		
18. partly		
19. belonged		

REVIEW

awoke	clever	lamb	real	stole
beef	eleven	nobody	saddle	sure
between	handle	paddle	Saturday	turtle
cattle	jar	provide	seat	wrong
cheer	job	quiet	seventh	yard

C. Farmyard Foul-ups Write Other Word Forms or the spelling words to complete these scenes that you may or may not see at a farm. Write each word or its Other Word Form only once. If you need help, use the **Spelling Dictionary**.

1. ants stuck to _ _ _ _ (jar) of honey spilled in the two _ _ _ _ _ (yard)

2. _ _ _ _ _ (seventh) ducks _ _ _ _ _ _ _ _ (paddle) backwards

3. shoes _ _ _ _ _ _ _ _ (provide) for horses but put on the _ _ _ _ _ (wrong) feet

4. children _ _ _ _ _ _ _ _ (handle) chicks _ _ _ _ _ _ _ (quiet)

5. baby _ _ _ _ _ (lamb) running _ _ _ _ _ _ _ (between) mother's legs

6. cooks _ _ _ _ _ _ _ _ (clever) spicing the _ _ _ _ (beef) for the noon meal

7. _ _ _ _ _ _ (real) dirty pigs that _ _ _ _ _ _ (nobody) wants to be near

8. children _ _ _ _ _ _ _ _ (cheer) for the _ _ _ _ _ _ _ (turtle) in the race

9. no _ _ _ _ _ (seat) for _ _ _ _ _ _ (eleven) hens to hatch their eggs

10. _ _ _ _ _ _ (cattle) being _ _ _ _ _ _ _ (saddle) for horses' _ _ _ _ (job)

11. a fox _ _ _ _ _ _ (sure) planning to return the _ _ _ _ _ _ (stole) eggs

12. roosters _ _ _ _ _ _ _ (awoke) early on a _ _ _ _ _ _ _ _ (Saturday)

alone	crack	harm	remind	steep
battle	drank	heel	shore	strong
chop	fled	indeed	smoke	tear
chose	fond	led	sob	tiny
coal	golden	monster	spoke	ton

D. Break the Code Use the code to write an Other Word Form or a spelling word.

1	2	3	4	5	6	7	8	9	10	11	12	13	14	15	16	17	18
↓	↓	↓	↓	↓	↓	↓	↓	↓	↓	↓	↓	↓	↓	↓	↓	↓	↓
a	b	c	d	e	f	g	h	i	k	l	m	n	o	p	r	s	t

1. ___ ___ ___ ___ ___ ___ ___
2 1 18 18 11 5 17

2. ___ ___ ___ ___ ___
11 5 1 4 17

3. ___ ___ ___ ___ ___ ___
9 13 4 5 5 4

4. ___ ___ ___ ___ ___ ___ ___ ___
6 14 13 4 13 5 17 17

5. ___ ___ ___ ___
6 11 5 5

6. ___ ___ ___ ___ ___ ___ ___ ___
17 18 16 14 13 7 5 16

7. ___ ___ ___ ___ ___
3 14 1 11 17

8. ___ ___ ___ ___ ___ ___ ___
18 9 13 9 5 17 18

9. ___ ___ ___ ___ ___ ___ ___
3 16 1 3 10 5 4

10. ___ ___ ___ ___ ___ ___ ___ ___
12 14 13 17 18 5 16 17

11. ___ ___ ___ ___ ___ ___ ___
17 12 14 10 9 13 7

12. ___ ___ ___ ___
18 14 13 17

13. ___ ___ ___ ___ ___ ___ ___
16 5 12 9 13 4 17

14. ___ ___ ___ ___ ___
18 5 1 16 17

15. ___ ___ ___ ___ ___ ___
17 15 14 10 5 13

16. ___ ___ ___ ___ ___
1 11 14 13 5

17. ___ ___ ___ ___ ___ ___ ___
17 14 2 2 9 13 7

18. ___ ___ ___ ___
7 14 11 4

19. ___ ___ ___ ___ ___ ___
17 8 14 16 5 17

20. ___ ___ ___ ___ ___ ___
8 1 16 12 5 4

21. ___ ___ ___ ___ ___
4 16 9 13 10

22. ___ ___ ___ ___ ___ ___
3 8 14 17 5 13

23. ___ ___ ___ ___ ___ ___ ___
3 8 14 15 15 5 4

24. ___ ___ ___ ___ ___ ___ ___ ___
17 18 5 5 15 5 17 18

25. ___ ___ ___ ___ ___
8 5 5 11 17

REVIEW

25

A. Pretest and Proofreading

B. Spelling Words and Phrases

1.	peek	to peek into the box
2.	queen	dressed like a queen
3.	sheet	a flowered sheet
4.	steel	steel rod
5.	wheel	behind the wheel
6.	sweep	to sweep into a pile
7.	sleepy	sleepy child
8.	flow	flow of the river
9.	slowly	crawled slowly
10.	throw	the longest throw
11.	grown	grown older
12.	shown	had shown me
13.	owner	found the owner
14.	hero	medal for the hero
15.	danger	sign of danger
16.	ranger	the ranger on duty
17.	strange	a strange sound
18.	change	too much change
19.	chance	not a chance
20.	dancing	dancing in a circle

Other Word Forms

peeked, peeking
queens, queenly
sheets
steels, steely
wheels, wheeled
swept, sweeping
sleep, sleeps, slept, sleepier, sleepiest
flows, flowed
slow, slowed, slower, slowest
threw, thrown
grow, grows, grew, growing
show, shows, showing
own, owns, owners
heroes
dangerous
range, ranges, ranged, ranging
stranger, strangest, strangely
changed, changing, changeable
chances
dance, dances

C. Visual Warm-up Write each word in its correct shape.

a.
b.
c.
d.
e.
f.
g.
h.
i.
j.
k.
l.
m.
n.
o.
p.
q.
r.
s.
t.

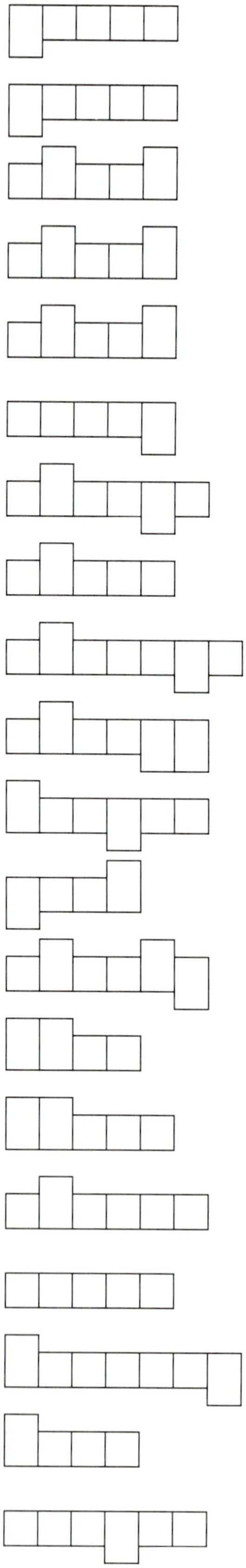

D. Three in a Row Write a spelling word for the group it best fits.

1. prince, king, ____________________
2. odd, weird, ____________________
3. tired, drowsy, ____________________
4. walking, skipping, ____________________
5. look, stare, ____________________
6. iron, brass, ____________________
7. buyer, seller, ____________________
8. shovel, rake, ____________________
9. catch, pitch, ____________________
10. blanket, towel, ____________________
11. harm, trouble, ____________________
12. winner, champion, ____________________

E. Scrambled Words Unscramble each scrambled word to find the spelling word that completes the sentence. Write the word.

1. We watched the gentle ____________________ (wofl) of the stream.
2. The bud had ____________________ (wnogr) into a flower.
3. We drove ____________________ (lslwoy) on the icy road.
4. The team had no ____________________ (acench) of winning.
5. The guide had ____________________ (ownsh) us the way.
6. Put a new ____________________ (elewh) on this bike.
7. Will you ____________________ (ngeach) the tire?
8. The forest ____________________ (ngrear) is in the tower.

Spelling Words

peek	queen	sheet	steel	wheel
sweep	sleepy	flow	slowly	throw
grown	shown	owner	hero	danger
ranger	strange	change	chance	dancing

F. Bases and Suffixes The spelling list contains thirteen base words and seven words with suffixes. Write each spelling word.

Words with Suffixes	Base Words	Words with Suffixes	Base Words
1. sweeping	________	**11.** wheeled	________
2. steely	________	**12.** peeking	________
3. heroes	________	**13.** dangerous	________
4. strangely	________	**14.** ________	slow
5. flowed	________	**15.** ________	range
6. changeable	________	**16.** ________	grow
7. queenly	________	**17.** ________	show
8. chances	________	**18.** ________	sleep
9. sheets	________	**19.** ________	dance
10. thrown	________	**20.** ________	own

G. Using Other Word Forms Write the Other Word Form that fits each group of words.

Base Words: throw(ew) sleepy(er) hero(es) change(ing) strange(ly)

1. good guys, idols, superstars, ____________
2. tossed, flung, passed, ____________
3. unusually, oddly, weirdly, ____________
4. replacing, swapping, switching, ____________
5. more tired, drowsier, more exhausted, ____________

H. Challenge Words Write the Challenge Word that fits each clue.

vocabulary	**deepest**	**detail**	**potato**	**measles**

1. can be mashed or fried ____________
2. like mumps or chicken pox ____________
3. a lot of words ____________
4. not at all shallow ____________
5. a fine point ____________

I. Spelling and Writing Write *two* or more answers to each question. Use as many Spelling Words, Other Word Forms, and Challenge Words as you can. A few words are suggested. Proofread your work.

1. What would you do to make sure that you did not get lost if you were hiking in a park or a forest?

   danger – ranger – change – detail

2. What would you do if you couldn't find your pet cat?

   peek – sheet – sleepy – shown – owner

3. What would you do if you walked into your house and found water leaking everywhere?

   sweep – flow – slowly – strange – deepest

26

A. Pretest and Proofreading

B. Spelling Words and Phrases

1.	shape	triangular shape
2.	hate	hate to be late
3.	lately	not lately
4.	making	making lunch
5.	lazy	felt very lazy
6.	sharing	sharing their toys
7.	careful	careful on a bike
8.	careless	careless around tools
9.	February	since February
10.	tend	tend to wait too long
11.	less	much less
12.	lesson	next lesson
13.	letting	letting me sing
14.	friends	some of my friends
15.	field	a field of daisies
16.	apiece	had three apiece
17.	fried	box of fried clams
18.	cried	cried softly
19.	lying	was caught lying
20.	nineteen	nineteen minutes

Other Word Forms

shapes, shaping
hates, hated, hateful
late, later, latest
make, makes, made
lazier, laziest
share, shares, shared
care, cares, caring, carelessness
Feb.
tends, tended, tending
little, lesser, least, lessen
lessons
let, lets
friend, friendly, friendship
fields
fry, fries, frying
cry, cries, crying
lie, lies, lied, liar
nineteenth

C. Visual Warm-up

Write each word in its correct shape.

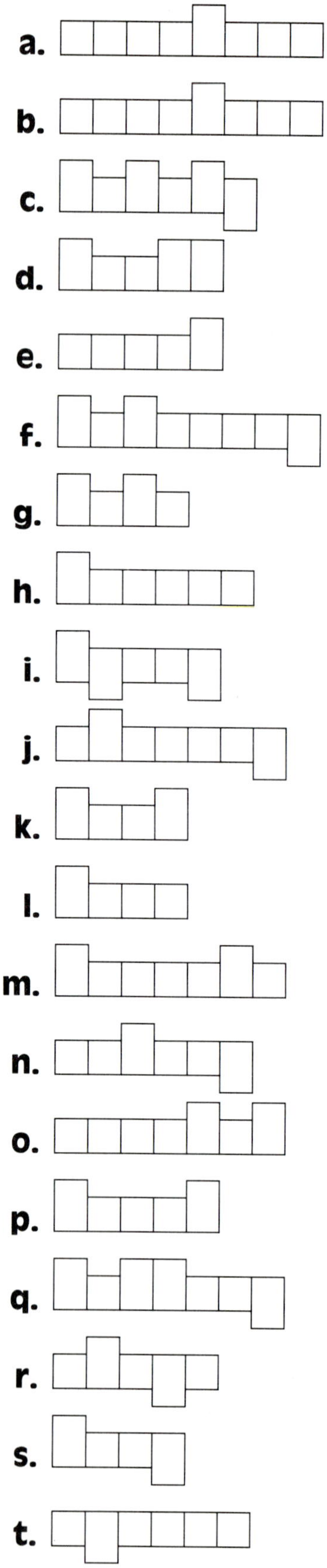

D. All in a Row Write the twenty spelling words in alphabetical order. Then join the boxed letters and write four hidden words.

1. _ ☐ _ _ _ _
2. _ _ _ ☐ _ _ _
3. _ ☐ _ _ _ _ _ _ _
4. ☐ _ _ _ _
5. _ ☐ _ _ _ _ _ _
6. Hidden Word: ____________
7. ☐ _ _ _ _
8. _ _ ☐ _ _
9. _ _ _ _ _ _ ☐
10. ☐ _ _ _
11. _ _ _ _ _ ☐
12. Hidden Word: ____________
13. _ ☐ _ _
14. ☐ _ _ _
15. ☐ _ _ _ _ _
16. _ ☐ _ _ _ _ _
17. _ ☐ _ _ _
18. Hidden Word: ____________
19. ☐ _ _ _ _ _
20. _ _ _ _ _ ☐ _ _
21. _ _ ☐ _ _
22. _ _ _ _ _ ☐ _
23. ☐ _ _ _
24. Hidden Word: ____________

E. Word Opposites Antonyms are word opposites. Write the antonym from the spelling list for each word or words below.

1. enemies ____________
2. more ____________
3. love ____________
4. busy ____________
5. careless ____________
6. truthful ____________
7. laughed ____________
8. careful ____________
9. long ago ____________

Spelling Words

shape	hate	lately	making	lazy
sharing	careful	careless	February	tend
less	lesson	letting	friends	field
apiece	fried	cried	lying	nineteen

F. Base Words The spelling list contains nine base words and eleven words that are not base words. Write each spelling word.

	Words That Are Not Base Words	Base Words		Words That Are Not Base Words	Base Words
1.	lessons	________	**11.**	________	lie
2.	fields	________	**12.**	________	friend
3.	shaping	________	**13.**	________	let
4.	nineteenth	________	**14.**	________	little
5.	tending	________	**15.**	________	care
6.	Feb.	________	**16.**	________	late
7.	laziest	________	**17.**	________	care
8.	hateful	________	**18.**	________	make
9.	________	fry	**19.**	________	share
10.	________	cry			

20. Write the one base word not used above. ________

G. Using Other Word Forms Write the Other Word Form that completes each question.

Base Words: lazy(er) friend(ship) shape(ing) lie(ar) fry(ing)

1. He told a lie. Was he a ________________?
2. They fried the potatoes. Did they use a ________________ pan?
3. They were good pals. Did they have a good ________________?
4. The dog was much more lazy. Was the dog ________________?
5. She was forming a ball of clay. Was she ________________ it with her hands?

H. Challenge Words Write the Challenge Word that completes each phrase.

petal	**checkers**	**spices**	**text**	**wages**

1. either chess or ________________
2. either salary or ________________
3. either seasoning or ________________
4. either a flower part or a ________________
5. either printed words or ________________

I. Spelling and Writing Write *two* or more answers to each question. Use as many Spelling Words, Other Word Forms, and Challenge Words as you can. A few words are suggested. Proofread your work.

1. What would you do if you arrived at a party and found that you knew only one person?

   careful – lesson – making – checkers

2. What would you think if you opened a beautifully wrapped birthday present and found that the box was empty?

   tend – sharing – careless – lying

3. What would you think if your friend served you soup on the hottest day of the summer?

   February – spices – lately – fried

27

A. Pretest and Proofreading

B. Spelling Words and Phrases

1.	**cabin**	cabin in the woods
2.	**magic**	a magic show
3.	**habit**	a good habit
4.	**blast**	blast of the rocket
5.	**basket**	threw it into the basket
6.	**absent**	never absent
7.	**fence**	painted the fence
8.	**sense**	makes lots of sense
9.	**cents**	forty-five cents
10.	**center**	open in the center
11.	**December**	December holiday
12.	**plenty**	plenty of time
13.	**twenty**	twenty miles to go
14.	**twenty-five**	twenty-five days
15.	**ripe**	almost ripe
16.	**likely**	likely to try again
17.	**sidewalk**	cement sidewalk
18.	**sideways**	sideways as a crab
19.	**fireplace**	in front of the fireplace
20.	**tired**	hot and tired

Other Word Forms

cabins
magical, magically, magician
habits
blasts, blasting
baskets
absently, absentee
fences, fenced, fencing
senses, sensed, sensing, senseless
cent
centers, centered, centering
Dec.
plentiful
twentieth
twenty-fifth
ripen, ripening, riper, ripest
like, likes, liked, liking
sidewalks
fireplace
tire, tires, tiring, tiresome, tireless

C. Visual Warm-up

Write each word in its correct shape.

a. b. c. d. e. f. g. h. i. j. k. l. m. n. o. p. q. r. s. t.

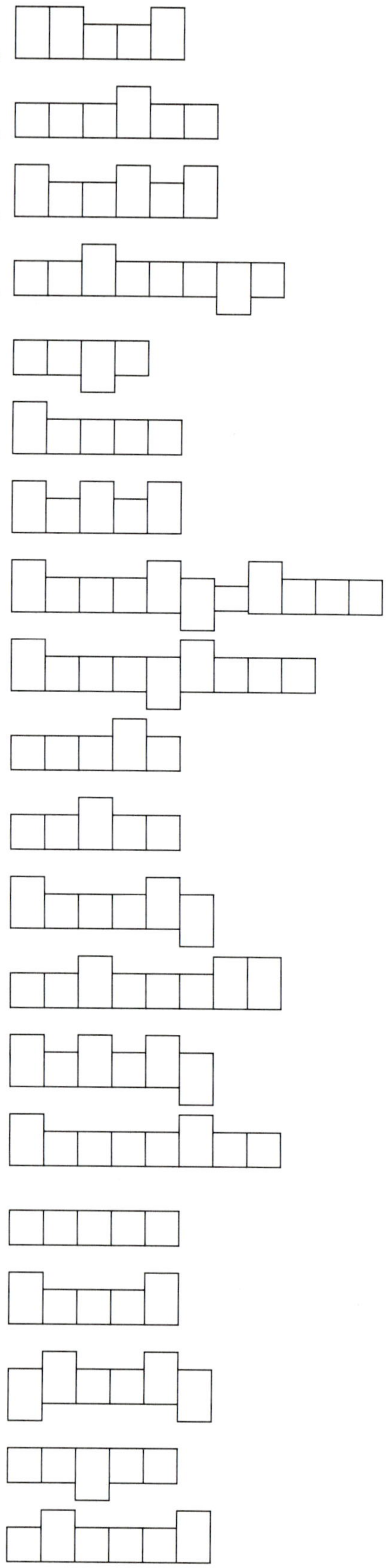

D. Missing Vowels Find the missing vowels and write the spelling words.

1. s __ ns __ __________
2. bl __ st __________
3. b __ sk __ t __________
4. h __ b __ t __________
5. f __ nc __ __________
6. t __ r __ d __________
7. r __ p __ __________
8. m __ g __ c __________
9. c __ nts __________
10. pl __ nt __ __________
11. tw __ nt __ __________
12. tw __ nt __ -f __ v __ __________
13. c __ b __ n __________
14. c __ nt __ r __________
15. __ bs __ nt __________
16. l __ k __ l __ __________
17. s __ d __ w __ __ s __________
18. D __ c __ mb __ r __________
19. f __ r __ pl __ c __ __________
20. s __ d __ w __ lk __________

E. Anagrams Change the letters around in these words and write the spelling words.

1. scent __________
2. tried __________
3. pier __________

F. Compound Words Join the eight words to write four compound words.

walk	side	ways	side
fire	five	twenty	place

1. __________
2. __________
3. __________
4. __________

Spelling Words

cabin	magic	habit	blast	basket
absent	fence	sense	cents	center
December	plenty	twenty	twenty-five	ripe
likely	sidewalk	sideways	fireplace	tired

G. Sound-alikes Write the two homophones from the spelling list.

1. ________________ **2.** ________________

H. Words and Meanings Write a spelling word for each meaning. Check your answers in the **Spelling Dictionary**.

1. a small, plain house ________________

2. the twelfth month of the year ________________

3. completely grown and ready for eating ________________

4. a wall that protects an area ________________

5. good judgment ________________

6. done by using tricks ________________

7. not present ________________

8. a full supply of all that's needed ________________

9. an explosion, or loud noise ________________

10. a place by the street where people can walk ________________

11. an opening that holds a fire ________________

12. a woven container ________________

13. an action repeated over and over ________________

14. half of fifty ________________

15. a few pennies ________________

16. with one side facing forward ________________

17. to be expected ________________

18. the middle part of something ________________

19. two times ten ________________

20. weary, or worn out ________________

I. Using Other Word Forms Write the Other Word Form that completes each sentence.

Base Words: absent(ee) plenty(ful) ripe(n) tire(ing) magic(ian)

1. The ________________ made the coin disappear.
2. This hard work is ________________ .
3. Water is ________________ in the ocean.
4. The banana must ________________ before you eat it.
5. The ________________ had to bring a written excuse.

J. Challenge Words Write the Challenge Word that completes each word pair.

hamburger	**cannon**	**retired**	**slender**	**tremble**

1. rifle or ________________
2. hot dog or ________________
3. thin or ________________
4. shiver or ________________
5. resigned or ________________

K. Spelling and Writing Read the story idea. Use the Spelling Words, Other Word Forms, and Challenge Words to help you think of an answer to each question. Proofread your work.

Story idea:
She awoke early on a typical December morning.

1. Who awoke early?
2. Why did she wake up early?
3. What were her plans for the day?
4. Where did this take place?
5. What did the place look like?
6. What made this a typical December day?

28

A. Pretest and Proofreading

B. Spelling Words and Phrases

1.	busy	should be busy
2.	build	would like to build
3.	built	built of bricks
4.	inch	just one more inch
5.	print	large, even print
6.	swing	high on the swing
7.	living	living next door
8.	aid	came to our aid
9.	afraid	afraid to enter
10.	chain	chain on the gate
11.	drain	will drain the water
12.	rainy	something for a rainy day
13.	mailed	mailed the letter
14.	waiting	waiting for the bus
15.	repair	will repair it soon
16.	oak	an oak table
17.	loads	loads of lumber
18.	roar	the roar of water
19.	board	balanced on the board
20.	floor	waxed the floor

Other Word Forms

- busier, busiest
- builds, building, builder
- inches, inched
- prints, printing, printer
- swings, swinging, swung
- live, lived
- aids, aided, aiding
- chains, chained, chaining
- drains, draining
- rain, rained, raining, rainier, rainiest
- mail, mails, mailing
- wait, waits, waited, waiter, waitress
- repairs, repaired, repairing
- oaks
- load, loaded, loading
- roars, roared, roaring
- boards, boarded, boarding, boarder
- floors

C. Visual Warm-up

Write each word in its correct shape.

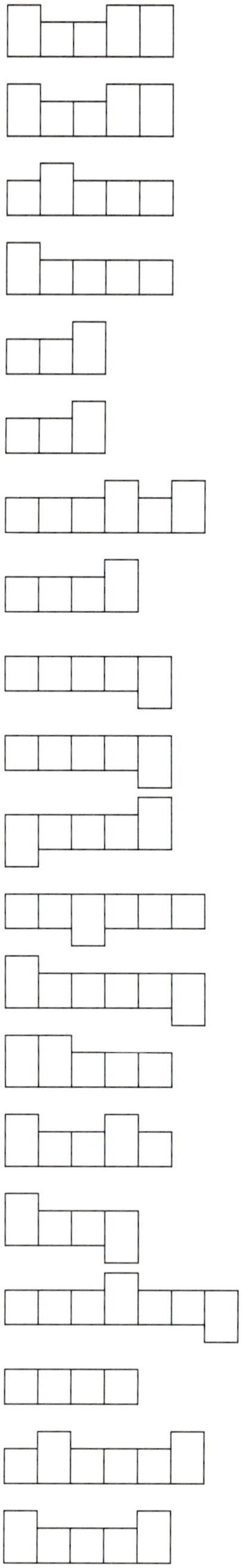

a. b. c. d. e. f. g. h. i. j. k. l. m. n. o. p. q. r. s. t.

D. Sort Your Words Write each spelling word in the correct column. Two words go in more than one column. Check your answers in the **Spelling Dictionary**.

Words with *ai*	Words with *oa*	Words with a Short *i* Sound
1. ________	9. ________	13. ________
2. ________	10. ________	14. ________
3. ________	11. ________	15. ________
4. ________	12. ________	16. ________
5. ________		17. ________
6. ________		18. ________
7. ________		19. ________
8. ________		20. ________
		21. ________

22. Write the word that did not fit in any column. ________

E. Base Words The spelling list contains fourteen base words and six words that are not base words. Write each spelling word.

	Words That Are Not Base Words	Base Words		Words That Are Not Base Words	Base Words
1.	oaks	________	11.	boarded	________
2.	chains	________	12.	inched	________
3.	building	________	13.	roaring	________
4.	busiest	________	14.	________	live
5.	repaired	________	15.	________	wait
6.	drains	________	16.	________	mail
7.	swinging	________	17.	________	load
8.	aided	________	18.	________	build
9.	floors	________	19.	________	rain
10.	printer	________			

20. Write the one base word not used above. ________

Spelling Words

busy	build	built	inch	print	swing
living	aid	afraid	chain	drain	rainy
mailed	waiting	repair	oak	loads	roar
board	floor				

F. Unscramble and Write Unscramble each scrambled word to find the spelling word that completes the sentence. Write the word.

1. I heard the _______________ (oarr) of the lion.
2. Did you _______________ (pearri) the broken wheel?
3. I'm not _______________ (daifra) of the dark.
4. Every _______________ (naich) has links.
5. I will _______________ (aindr) the soapy water.
6. My cousin _______________ (laimed) the letter.
7. Bees are _______________ (suby) insects.
8. Did you _______________ (lduib) a snow fort?
9. We must _______________ (ntipr) our names.
10. They carried many _______________ (doals) of books.
11. Today is a _______________ (niray) day.
12. No _______________ (dia) is needed to finish the job.
13. The house was _______________ (ltibu) in 1860.
14. The _______________ (ngisw) needs a new seat.
15. There are elm and _______________ (koa) trees in our yard.
16. We are _______________ (angwiti) for a friend.
17. An _______________ (chni) is smaller than a foot.
18. One oak _______________ (bardo) is all we need.
19. A wool rug covers the _______________ (roflo).
20. My sister is _______________ (ingvil) in Texas.

G. Using Other Word Forms Write the Other Word Form that completes each sentence.

Base Words: rainy(er) board(ing) wait(r)(ess) busy(est) repair(ed)

1. No one was as busy as my brother. He was the ________________ .
2. It rained more today than yesterday. Today is ________________ .
3. She served our meal. She was our ________________ .
4. She fixed the bicycle. The bike is now ________________ .
5. The pirates were coming onto the ship. They were ________________ it.

H. Challenge Words Write the Challenge Word that completes each sentence.

cardboard	**thrilling**	**distance**	**erase**	**therefore**

1. We traveled a long ________________ .
2. Use heavy paper or ________________ .
3. I'm your friend; ________________ , you can count on me.
4. The roller coaster is a ________________ ride.
5. I'll ________________ the chalkboard.

I. Spelling and Writing Write *two* or more answers to each question. Use as many Spelling Words, Other Word Forms, and Challenge Words as you can. A few words are suggested. Proofread your work.

1. What would you do if your tree house was ruined in a bad wind storm?

   busy – build – repair – board – oak

2. What would you do if you were the only survivor after a shipwreck?

   afraid – rainy – living – aid – thrilling

3. What would you want to know before entering a poster-drawing contest?

   print – inch – mailed – erase – cardboard

29

A. Pretest and Proofreading

B. Spelling Words and Phrases

1.	sack	sack of potatoes
2.	cash	to cash a check
3.	mask	a plain black mask
4.	gang	tried to gang up
5.	demand	to demand a reply
6.	grandmother	grandmother and aunt
7.	basketball	a game of basketball
8.	none	but there were none
9.	front	through the front door
10.	above	above them all
11.	month	one month later
12.	Monday	on a rainy Monday
13.	honey	honey from the hive
14.	discover	tried to discover
15.	recover	will recover my breath
16.	thousand	a thousand times
17.	amount	very small amount
18.	around	around the next corner
19.	bound	bound with rope
20.	wound	wound around their legs

Other Word Forms

sacks
cashes, cashed, cashing, cashier
masks, masked, masking
gangs
demands, demanded, demanding
grandmothers
basketballs
front
months, monthly
Mon.
honeys, honeyed
discovers, discovered, discovering, discoverer, discovery
recovers, recovered, recovering, recovery
thousands, thousandth
amounts, amounted, amounting
bind, binds, binding
wind, winding

C. Visual Warm-up

Write each word in its correct shape.

a. b. c. d. e. f. g. h. i. j. k. l. m. n. o. p. q. r. s. t.

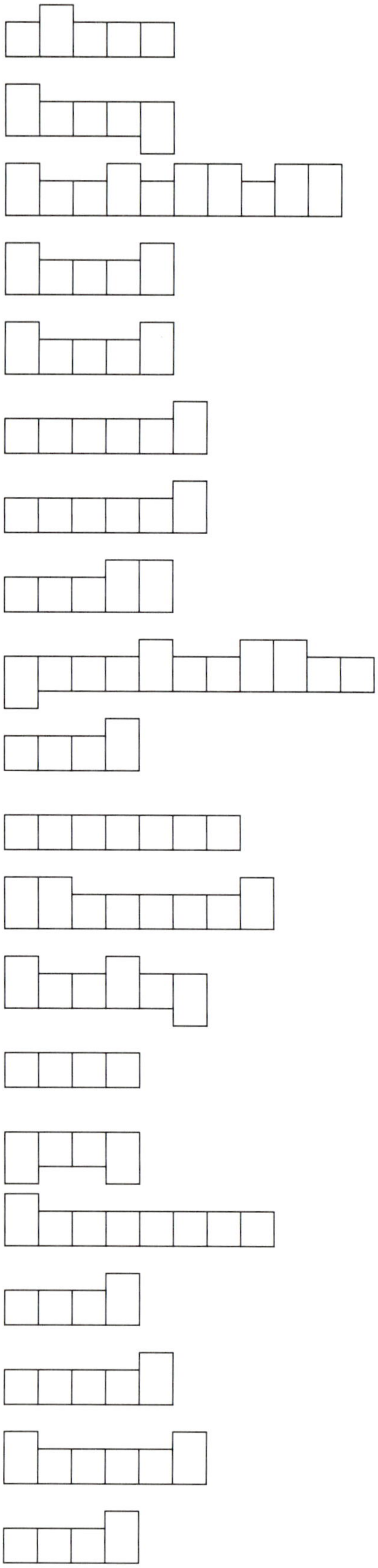

D. Sort Your Words

1. Write the seven words with a short *a* sound. Check your answers in the **Spelling Dictionary**. Circle the two letters that follow the letter that spells the short *a* sound.

______ ______ ______

______ ______ ______

______

2. Write the words with a short *u* sound.

______ ______ ______

______ ______ ______

______ ______ ______

3. What letter spells the short *u* sound? ______

4. Write the five words with the *ou* sound as in *ouch*. Circle the word that could also have the *oo* sound as in *boot*.

______ ______ ______

______ ______

5. Write the two compound words.

______ ______

E. Not This, but That

Write spelling words to complete the phrases below.

1. not a check, but ______
2. not Sunday, but ______
3. not below, but ______
4. not between, but ______
5. not a costume, but a ______
6. not grandfather, but ______
7. not a basket, but a ______
8. not many, but ______
9. not hundred, but ______
10. not back, but ______
11. not ask, but ______
12. not sugar, but ______
13. not one, but a ______
14. not year, but ______
15. not a part, but an ______
16. not hide, but ______
17. not baseball, but ______
18. not lose, but ______
19. not untied, but ______
20. not unwound, but ______

Spelling Words

sack	cash	mask	gang	demand
grandmother	basketball	none	front	above
month	Monday	honey	discover	recover
thousand	amount	around	bound	wound

F. Crossword Puzzle Solve the puzzle by using words from the spelling list. Write the words. Check your answers in the **Spelling Dictionary**.

Across

1. a sport played on a court
4. a large group
6. money
8. to ask for strongly
10. ten times one hundred
12. a day of the week
14. not any
15. part of a year
16. to get back something lost
17. the part facing forward
18. in a circle

Down

1. tied
2. a bag
3. the total
5. your father's mother
7. a liquid made by bees
9. wrapped around
11. not below
13. to find out for the first time
15. a face covering

G. Using Other Word Forms Write the Other Word Form that answers each question.

Base Words: thousand(th) recover(y) discover(y) cash(ier) month(ly)

1. Who collects the money at the store? ______________________

2. How often does the calendar need to be changed? ______________________

3. What follows the nine hundred ninety-ninth? ______________________

4. What did Christopher Columbus hope to make? ______________________

5. What does a hospital patient hope to make? ______________________

H. Challenge Words Write the Challenge Word that completes each word pair.

couches	crumbled	cloudy	halves	shoved

1. shattered and ______________________

2. rainy and ______________________

3. wholes and ______________________

4. pushed and ______________________

5. sofas and ______________________

I. Spelling and Writing Read the story idea. Use the Spelling Words, Other Word Forms, and Challenge Words to help you think of an answer to each question. Proofread your work.

Story idea:
As he reached for the honey, the buzzing sounds became louder.

1. Who reached for the honey?

2. What made the buzzing sounds?

3. Why did the noise become louder?

4. How did the main character feel about the noise?

5. Where did this happen?

6. When did this happen?

30 REVIEWING LESSONS 25-29

■	★	▲	◆	●
grown	cried	dancing	bound	lesson
field	cents	friends	basket	fireplace
build	loads	wound	rainy	mailed
honey	waiting	above	gang	grandmother
throw	month	fried	lazy	afraid

A. Words in a Series Use Other Word Forms or the spelling words to complete each series. The shapes tell you in what column you can find the spelling word. Use each word or its Other Word Form only once.

1. groups, crowds, ◆ __ __ __ __ __

2. moves, steps, ▲ __ __ __ __ __ __

3. bees, sweetener, ■ __ __ __ __ __

4. days, weeks, ★ __ __ __ __ __ __

5. shower, sprinkle, ◆ __ __ __ __

6. pal, person, ▲ __ __ __ __ __ __

7. pastures, meadows, ■ __ __ __ __ __ __

8. sobbing, weeping, ★ __ __ __ __ __ __

9. stayed, rested, ★ __ __ __ __ __ __

10. buckets, boxes, ◆ __ __ __ __ __ __ __

11. making, stacking, ■ __ __ __ __ __ __ __ __

12. cooking, browning, ▲ __ __ __ __ __ __

13. frightened, scared, ● __ __ __ __ __ __

14. filling, packing, ★ __ __ __ __ __ __ __

15. assignments, exercises, ● __ __ __ __ __ __ __

16. becoming, raising, ■ __ __ __ __ __ __ __

17. overhead, higher, ▲ __ __ __ __ __

18. tossing, pitching, ■ __ __ __ __ __ __ __ __

19. chimneys, hearths, ● __ __ __ __ __ __ __ __ __ __

20. person, relative, ● __ __ __ __ __ __ __ __ __ __ __

21. tied, knotted, ◆ __ __ __ __ __

22. penny, coin, ★ __ __ __ __

23. wrap, coil, ▲ __ __ __ __

24. tired, slow, ◆ __ __ __ __

25. send, postmark, ● __ __ __ __

REVIEW

absent	December	letting	plenty	sideways
busy	February	likely	ranger	steel
careful	front	Monday	ripe	strange
careless	hero	none	sack	sweep
danger	less	owner	sidewalk	tired

B. Bag of Words Find the missing letters and write the Other Word Forms. If you need help, use the **Spelling Dictionary**.

The *s* Bag

1. s __ __ __ __ s ________

2. o __ __ __ __ s ________

3. r __ __ __ __ __ s ________

4. d __ __ __ __ __ s ________

5. l __ __ s ________

6. s __ __ __ __ __ __ __ s ________

7. t __ __ __ s ________

8. l __ __ __ s ________

9. f __ __ __ __ s ________

10. s __ __ __ s ________

11. s __ __ __ __ s ________

The *er* Bag

18. l __ __ __ er ________

19. r __ __ er ________

20. b __ __ __ er ________

The *es* Bag

21. h __ __ __ es ________

The Empty Bag

Write the two words that have no Other Word Forms.

12. s __ __ __ __ __ __ __ ________

13. n __ __ __ ________

The *ful* Bag

22. p __ __ __ __ __ __ ful ________

The *ly* Bag

14. c __ __ __ __ __ __ __ ly ________

15. s __ __ __ __ __ __ ly ________

16. a __ __ __ __ __ ly ________

17. c __ __ __ __ __ __ __ ly ________

The Abbreviation Bag

23. F __ __ . ________

24. M __ __ . ________

25. D __ __ . ________

REVIEW

■	★	▲	◆	●
slowly	sharing	drain	twenty	oak
sheet	making	nineteen	built	thousand
queen	lately	cabin	swing	around
sleepy	apiece	magic	floor	basketball
shown	lying	habit	living	twenty-five

C. What a Feeling! Write Other Word Forms or the spelling words to complete these ideas that could make you feel good. The shapes tell you in what column you can find the spelling word. Write each word or its Other Word Form only once. If you need help, use the **Spelling Dictionary**.

1. playing ● ___ ___ ___ ___ ___ ___ ___ ___ ___ ___ on a warm spring day
2. pretending to be a ■ ___ ___ ___ ___ ___ who ◆ ___ ___ ___ ___ ___ in a castle
3. getting into a bed freshly ★ ___ ___ ___ ___ with clean ■ ___ ___ ___ ___ ___ ___
4. finding only ● ___ ___ ___ ___ ___ ___ ___ ___ ___ ___ questions instead of one ● ___ ___ ___ ___ ___ ___ ___ ___ on your math test.
5. ◆ ___ ___ ___ ___ ___ ___ ___ ___ a fence ● ___ ___ ___ ___ ___ ___ your garden
6. smelling the pine ◆ ___ ___ ___ ___ ___ ___ in a summer ▲ ___ ___ ___ ___ ___
7. ■ ___ ___ ___ ___ ___ ___ ___ a ▲ ___ ___ ___ ___ ___ trick and having it work
8. waking your ■ ___ ___ ___ ___ ___ ___ ___ ___ brother so he isn't ★ ___ ___ ___ ___ for school
9. selling your homemade bookmarks for ◆ ___ ___ ___ ___ ___ ___ cents ★ ___ ___ ___ ___ ___ ___ at the school fair
10. having ▲ ___ ___ ___ ___ ___ ___ ___ ___ cookies to ★ ___ ___ ___ ___ ___
11. having your teacher say that your study ▲ ___ ___ ___ ___ ___ ___ have ■ ___ ___ ___ ___ ___ ___ improved
12. ◆ ___ ___ ___ ___ ___ ___ ___ ___ on a tire under the ● ___ ___ ___ tree
13. finding out that your friend did not ★ ___ ___ ___ to you
14. fixing the clogged ▲ ___ ___ ___ ___ ___ in the kitchen sink

REVIEW

change	peek	center	aid	mask
hate	tend	roar	shape	repair
chance	blast	board	demand	recover
wheel	sense	chain	amount	print
flow	fence	inch	cash	discover

D. Word Building Add word parts to each spelling word to make Other Word Forms. If you need help, use the **Spelling Dictionary**.

Spelling Words	*s* or *es*	*ed*	*ing*
Example: walk	*walks*	*walked*	*walking*
1. blast			
2. chain			
3. hate			
4. peek			
5. aid			
6. print			
7. change			
8. fence			
9. demand			
10. mask			
11. tend			
12. center			
13. amount			
14. repair			
15. wheel			
16. sense			
17. inch			
18. shape			
19. recover			
20. flow			
21. roar			
22. cash			
23. board			
24. chance			
25. discover			

REVIEW

31

A. Pretest and Proofreading

B. Spelling Words and Phrases

1. pool	jumped into the pool
2. loop	loop in the rope
3. root	root of the plant
4. tooth	chipped a front tooth
5. bloom	will bloom in spring
6. speak	when you speak
7. dream	unusual dream
8. feast	the holiday feast
9. beast	beast in the jungle
10. cable	a new cable car
11. stable	cleaning the stable
12. paste	wallpaper paste
13. waste	threw away the waste
14. attic	in the dusty attic
15. address	new address
16. happening	happening to me
17. sitting	sitting very straight
18. bigger	not much bigger
19. pillow	fluffed up the pillow
20. middle	middle of the night

Other Word Forms

pools
loops, looped, looping
roots, rooted, rooting
teeth, toothy
blooms, bloomed, blooming
speaks, spoke, spoken, speaking
dreams, dreamed, dreaming, dreamer, dreamt
feasts, feasted, feasting
beasts, beastly
cables, cabled
stables, stabled
pastes, pasted, pasting
wastes, wasted, wasting, wasteful
attics
addresses, addressed
happen, happens, happened
sit, sits, sat
big, biggest
pillows

C. Visual Warm-up

Write each word in its correct shape.

a. b. c. d. e. f. g. h. i. j. k. l. m. n. o. p. q. r. s. t.

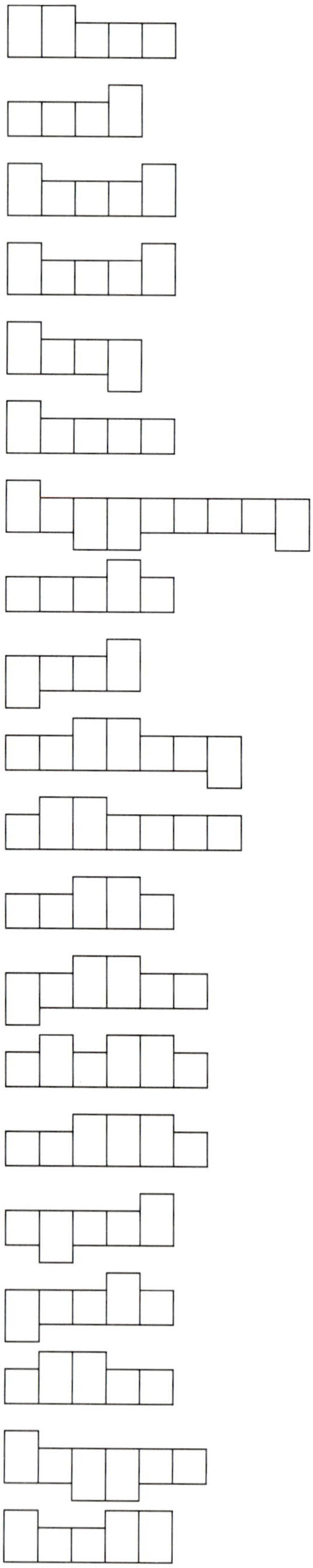

D. Sort Your Words In alphabetical order, write the spelling words where they belong.

Words with Double Consonants	Words with Double Vowels
1. ________	12. ________
2. ________	13. ________
3. ________	14. ________
4. ________	15. ________
5. ________	16. ________
6. ________	
7. ________	
Words with a Long *a* Sound	**Words with a Long *e* Sound**
8. ________	17. ________
9. ________	18. ________
10. ________	19. ________
11. ________	20. ________

E. Word Relatives Write the word from the spelling list that is related to each word or words below.

1. garbage ________
2. animal ________
3. nightmare ________
4. street ________
5. ribbon ________
6. flower ________
7. talk ________
8. taking place ________
9. bed ________
10. carrot ________
11. chew ________
12. top floor ________
13. center ________
14. chair ________
15. glue ________
16. meal ________
17. larger ________
18. barn ________
19. swimming ________
20. rope ________

Spelling Words

pool	loop	root	tooth	bloom
speak	dream	feast	beast	cable
stable	paste	waste	attic	address
happening	sitting	bigger	pillow	middle

F. Guide Words These word pairs are guide words that might appear in a dictionary. Write the words from the spelling list that would appear on the same page as each pair of guide words.

above – ax

1. ________________
2. ________________

backward – blade

3. ________________
4. ________________

blame – bucket

5. ________________

build – change

6. ________________

dirty – evening

7. ________________

event – flock

8. ________________

get – hate

9. ________________

leaf – lucky

10. ________________

mean – nineteen

11. ________________

outfits – plum

12. ________________
13. ________________

pocket – purse

14. ________________

returning – saves

15. ________________

shell – sitting

16. ________________

sob – straw

17. ________________
18. ________________

throw – unlock

19. ________________

until – worry

20. ________________

G. Using Other Word Forms Write the Other Word Form that fits each series.

Base Words: paste(ing) dream(ed) waste(ing) root(ed) feast(ing)

1. feasts, feasted, ________________
2. pastes, pasted, ________________
3. wastes, wasted, ________________
4. dreams, ________________, dreaming
5. roots, ________________, rooting

H. Challenge Words Write the Challenge Word that fits each group of words.

juice	**canteen**	**abandon**	**salmon**	**visiting**

1. spawn, swim upstream, fish, ________________
2. camping, water, container, ________________
3. guests, drop in, calling on, ________________
4. leave behind, give up, leave alone, ________________
5. orange, breakfast, liquid, ________________

I. Spelling and Writing Read the paragraph. Use as many Spelling Words, Other Word Forms, and Challenge Words as you can to write *two* or more answers to each question. Proofread your work.

Taku Lodge is a great place to visit in Alaska, especially when the weather is warm. In summer, the lodge sits in the middle of a meadow of blooming flowers, surrounded by evergreen forests and icy glaciers. Many people come to Taku Lodge to fish and to feast on Alaskan salmon. Some people just like to relax inside and watch the large bears that come to the lodge in search of food. Visitors may have different reasons for first coming to Taku Lodge, but they all dream of returning another time.

1. What is Taku Lodge like?
2. Why do different people enjoy visiting Taku Lodge?

32

A. Pretest and Proofreading

B. Spelling Words and Phrases

1.	color	a bright color
2.	among	among their friends
3.	another	to one another
4.	anybody	if anybody knows
5.	follow	tried to follow
6.	gotten	had gotten lost
7.	October	cool October day
8.	orange	peeled the orange
9.	beat	a beat of the drum
10.	means	whatever it means
11.	reader	the next reader
12.	season	in any season
13.	leaving	leaving shortly
14.	nearest	to the nearest phone
15.	ray	a ray of sunshine
16.	May	in the month of May
17.	playmate	with my playmate
18.	always	always smiling
19.	sank	sank into the sea
20.	fallen	a fallen apple

Other Word Forms

colors, coloring
amongst
follows, followed, following, follower
get, gets, got, getting
Oct.
oranges
beats, beaten, beating
mean, meant, meaning
read, reads, reading
seasons, seasonal
leave, leaves, left
near, nearer, nearly
rays
playmates
sink, sinks, sunk, sinking
fall, falls, fell, falling

C. Visual Warm-up

Write each word in its correct shape.

a.

b.

c.

d.

e.

f.

g.

h.

i.

j.

k.

l.

m.

n.

o.

p.

q.

r.

s.

t.

D. Missing Vowels Find the missing vowels and write the spelling words.

1. g ___ tt ___ n ______________
2. m ___ ___ ns ______________
3. f ___ ll ___ w ______________
4. c ___ l ___ r ______________
5. r ___ ___ ______________
6. ___ m ___ ng ______________
7. s ___ nk ______________
8. f ___ ll ___ n ______________
9. b ___ ___ t ______________
10. M ___ ___ ______________
11. ___ r ___ ng ___ ______________
12. ___ lw ___ ___ s ______________
13. ___ ct ___ b ___ r ______________
14. r ___ ___ d ___ r ______________
15. n ___ ___ r ___ st ______________
16. pl ___ ___ m ___ t ___ ______________
17. ___ n ___ th ___ r ______________
18. ___ n ___ b ___ d ___ ______________
19. l ___ ___ v ___ ng ______________
20. s ___ ___ s ___ n ______________

E. Hideaway Words from the spelling list are hiding in the underlined words in each sentence. Circle the words. Write the words.

1. Spring and fall entice many tourists to the mountains. *fallen*
2. Can you display material for the sale? ______________
3. The captain sailed the seas on a ship. ______________
4. Bankers dread errors being made in money matters. ______________
5. The tube attached to the beaker is broken. ______________
6. The skater's ankle was swollen ______________
7. The boss knows several ways to solve problems. ______________
8. The farmer fears no ranges will be left for cattle. ______________
9. The extra yam must be eaten. ______________
10. He turns on that spigot ten times a day. ______________
11. That dog is a mongrel. ______________
12. Please give me answers to the questions. ______________
13. Walk by the sea not here by the dunes. ______________
14. Gone are stories of the wild West. ______________

Spelling Words

color	among	another	anybody	follow
gotten	October	orange	beat	means
reader	season	leaving	nearest	ray
May	playmate	always	sank	fallen

F. Base Words The spelling list contains thirteen base words and seven words that are not base words. Write each spelling word.

Words That Are Not Base Words	Base Words
1. coloring	______
2. rays	______
3. seasonal	______
4. follower	______
5. beaten	______
6. Oct.	______
7. playmates	______
8. oranges	______

Words That Are Not Base Words	Base Words
9. ______	fall
10. ______	sink
11. ______	mean
12. ______	near
13. ______	read
14. ______	get
15. ______	leave

16. Write the five words not used above. ______ ______ ______ ______ ______

G. Using Other Word Forms Write the Other Word Form that completes each sentence.

Base Words: beat(en) near(ly) season(al) follow(ing) mean(t)

1. It was almost twelve o'clock. It was ______________ noon.

2. He was behind her. He was ______________ her.

3. The eggs and milk were mixed together. They were ______________ .

4. He was serious about what he said. He really ______________ it.

5. It happens every spring. It is a ______________ celebration.

H. Challenge Words Write the Challenge Word that completes each sentence.

raiders	**country**	**hauled**	**pioneers**	**beneath**

1. If they're not colonists, they may be ______________ .

2. If they're not on top, they may be ______________ .

3. If they're not invaders, they may be ______________ .

4. If it's not a continent, it may be a ______________ .

5. If it's not carried, it may be ______________ .

I. Spelling and Writing Write each set of words in a sentence. You may use Other Word Forms. Proofread your work.

1. May – October

2. playmate – leaving

3. always – gotten

4. ray – color

5. another – reader

6. anybody – means

7. season – follow

8. orange – fallen

9. among – beat

10. nearest – sank

11. country – pioneers

12. hauled – beneath

13. raiders – followed

33

A. Pretest and Proofreading

B. Spelling Words and Phrases

1.	born	born nine years ago
2.	fork	fork of the tree
3.	fort	built a snow fort
4.	forty	forty winks
5.	corner	piled in the corner
6.	before	before you're through
7.	fourth	the fourth grade
8.	fourteen	fourteen years old
9.	pouring	pouring from the pitcher
10.	silk	made of silk
11.	sink	dishes in the sink
12.	kick	a long, hard kick
13.	rich	a rich person
14.	film	watched the film
15.	windy	high on a windy hill
16.	enjoy	for you to enjoy
17.	second	in just one second
18.	pretend	when they pretend
19.	correct	correct time
20.	baseball	baseball cards

Other Word Forms

forks, forked
forts
fortieth
corners, cornered, cornering
four
fourteenth
pour, pours, poured
silky, silken
sinks, sinking, sank, sunk, sunken
kicks, kicked, kicking
richer, richest, richly
films, filmed, filming
wind, windier, windiest
enjoys, enjoyed, enjoying
seconds, seconded, seconding
pretends, pretending, pretended, pretender
corrects, corrected, correcting
baseballs

C. Visual Warm-up

Write each word in its correct shape.

a. b. c. d. e. f. g. h. i. j. k. l. m. n. o. p. q. r. s. t.

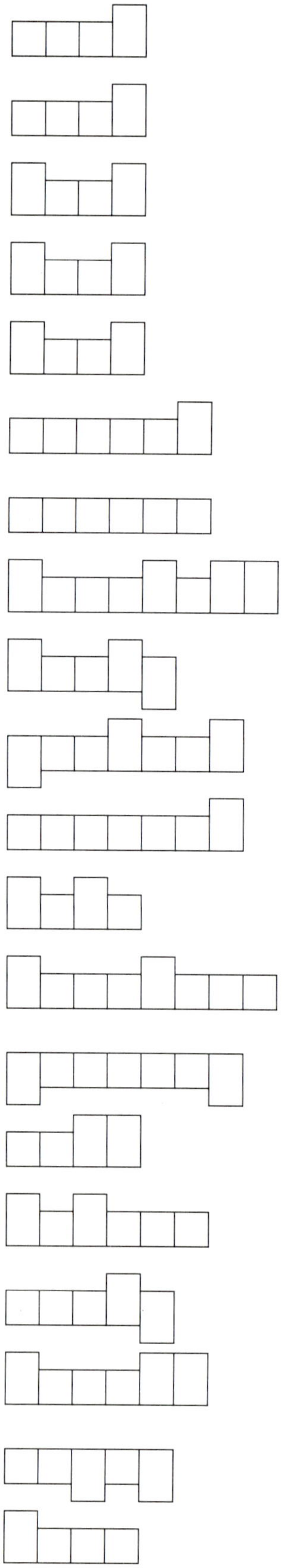

D. Sort Your Words In alphabetical order, write the spelling words under the correct headings. One word goes under two headings.

Words with *or* or *our*

1. ______ 5. ______ 9. ______
2. ______ 6. ______ 10. ______
3. ______ 7. ______
4. ______ 8. ______

Words in Which *i* Is Followed by Two Consonants

11. ______ 14. ______ 16. ______
12. ______ 15. ______ 17. ______
13. ______

18. Write the one compound word. ______

19. Write the three spelling words you have not used. ______

______ ______

E. Three in a Row Write a spelling word for the group it best fits.

1. edge, end, ______
2. velvet, satin, ______
3. ______, during, after
4. knife, spoon, ______
5. serving, flowing, ______
6. stormy, rainy, ______
7. stove, refrigerator, ______
8. make-believe, fake, ______
9. football, basketball, ______
10. cartoon, movie, ______
11. life, baby, ______
12. ______, fifty, sixty
13. love, like, ______
14. second, third, ______
15. money, wealthy, ______
16. ______, fifteen, sixteen
17. building, castle, ______
18. run, pass, ______
19. first, ______, third
20. OK, right, ______

Spelling Words

born	fork	fort	forty	corner	before
fourth	fourteen	pouring	silk	sink	kick
rich	film	windy	enjoy	second	pretend
correct	baseball				

F. Guide Words These word pairs are guide words that might appear in a dictionary. Write the words from the spelling list that would appear on the same page as each pair of guide words.

backward – blade

1. ____________
2. ____________

blame – bucket

3. ____________

chart – corner

4. ____________

correct – dirt

5. ____________

dirty – evening

6. ____________

event – flock

7. ____________

floor – gang

8. ____________
9. ____________
10. ____________
11. ____________
12. ____________

kick – leading

13. ____________

pocket – purse

14. ____________
15. ____________

returning – saves

16. ____________

scale – sheet

17. ____________

shell – sitting

18. ____________
19. ____________

until – worry

20. ____________

G. Using Other Word Forms Write the Other Word Form that answers each question.

Base Words: fourteen(th) rich(est) silk(y) forty(eth) pretend(ing)

1. What comes after the thirty-ninth? the ____________

2. Who is the person with the most money? the ____________

3. How did the new dress feel? ____________

4. What is the faker doing? ____________

5. What date followed the thirteenth? the ____________

H. Challenge Words Write the Challenge Word that completes each phrase.

adore	**complain**	**rebels**	**orphans**	**kisses**

1. not followers, but ____________

2. not hugs, but ____________

3. not agree, but ____________

4. not dislike, but ____________

5. not children with parents, but ____________

I. Spelling and Writing Read the paragraph. Use as many Spelling Words, Other Word Forms, and Challenge Words as you can to write *two* or more answers to each question. Proofread your work.

Roberto Clemente was born in Puerto Rico. Before his career as a professional player with the Pittsburgh Pirates, he worked hard to become great at baseball. As a professional player, he made lots of money and had thousands of adoring fans. Clemente enjoyed using his money to help children, especially those without families. He poured much of his money into a "sports city" for the children of Puerto Rico. Anyone who knew Clemente would agree that he always tried to do the right things in life.

1. What do you know about Roberto Clemente's early life?

2. What did Clemente do after he became a professional baseball player?

34

A. Pretest and Proofreading

B. Spelling Words and Phrases

1.	huge	a huge snowdrift
2.	June	was finished last June
3.	July	Fourth of July
4.	rules	set of rules
5.	woman	next to the woman
6.	ounce	sold by the ounce
7.	pound	89¢ a pound
8.	count	to count them again
9.	mouse	signs of a mouse
10.	hour	an hour ago
11.	flour	ground into flour
12.	steam	steam from the kettle
13.	stream	rushing stream
14.	scream	frightened scream
15.	sneakers	brand-new sneakers
16.	inches	measured in inches
17.	since	since 1874
18.	picnic	picnic basket
19.	picture	hung the picture
20.	single	in a single file

Other Word Forms

hugest, hugeness
rule, ruled, ruling, ruler
women, womanly
ounces, oz.
pounds, lb.
counts, counted, counting, counter
mice
hours, hourly, hr.
flours
steams, steamer
streams
screams, screamed, screaming
sneaker
inch, inched, inching, in.
picnics, picnicking
pictures, pictured, picturing
singly

C. Visual Warm-up

Write each word in its correct shape.

a.
b.
c.
d.
e.
f.
g.
h.
i.
j.
k.
l.
m.
n.
o.
p.
q.
r.
s.
t.

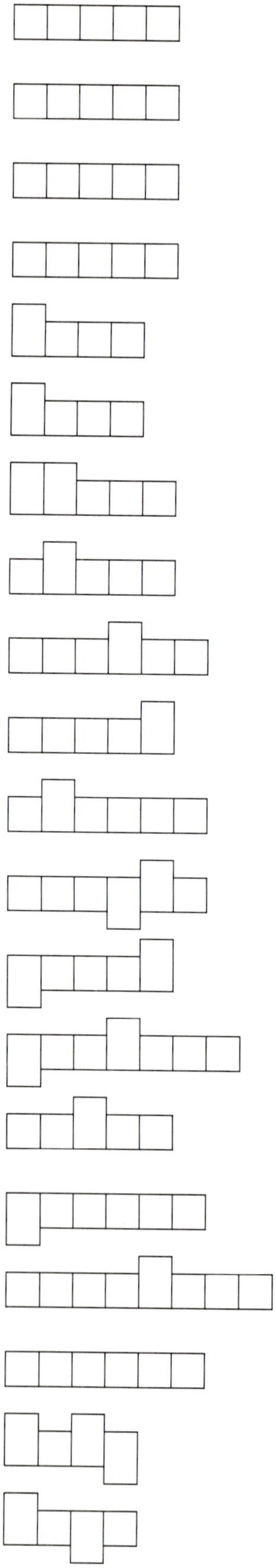

D. Sort Your Words

1. Find the missing letters to make spelling words. Write the words.

a. mou ___ ___ ____________________

b. ___ ___ ou ___ ____________________

c. pou ___ ___ ____________________

d. ou ___ ___ ___ ____________________

e. ___ ou ___ ____________________

f. cou ___ ___ ____________________

g. How are all these words alike? ____________________

____

2. Find the missing letters to make spelling words. Write the words.

a. ___ t ___ ea ___ ____________________

b. ___ ___ rea ___ ____________________

c. ___ ___ ea ___ ___ ___ ___ ____________________

d. ___ ___ ea ___ ____________________

3. Write the five spelling words that have a short *i* sound.

____________________ ____________________

____________________ ____________________

____

4. Write the five spelling words you did not write above.

____________________ ____________________

____________________ ____________________

____

E. For Short Write the spelling word or Other Word Form (p. 136) for each abbreviation.

1. hr. ____________________ **3.** lb. ____________________

2. oz. ____________________ **4.** in. ____________________

Spelling Words

huge June July rules woman ounce
pound count mouse hour flour steam
stream scream sneakers inches since picnic
picture single

F. Solve the Puzzle Solve the puzzle by using words from the spelling list. Write the words. Check your answers in the **Spelling Dictionary**.

Across

3. used in baking
4. sixteen ounces
5. a small animal
6. to add up
10. from that time
11. a loud cry
13. the sixth month
15. laws
16. twelve in a foot
17. hot mist
18. gym shoes

Down

1. sixty minutes
2. large
4. an outdoor meal
7. a measure of weight
8. one
9. an adult female
12. a brook
13. the seventh month
14. a drawing

G. Using Other Word Forms Add an ending to each word to write an Other Word Form.

Base Words: picture(ing) picnic(ing) scream(ing) count(ing) rule(ing)

1. rule + ing = ______________
2. scream + ing = ______________
3. count + ing = ______________
4. picture + ing = ______________
5. picnic + ing = ______________

H. Challenge Words Write the Challenge Word that completes each sentence.

indent	butcher	beetle	believe	scooped

1. Once I was a meat packer; now I'm a ______________ .
2. Once I saw an ant; now I see a ______________ .
3. Once I doubted you; now I ______________ you.
4. Once I wrote beside the margin; now I ______________ each paragraph.
5. Once the sherbet was spooned; now it is ______________ .

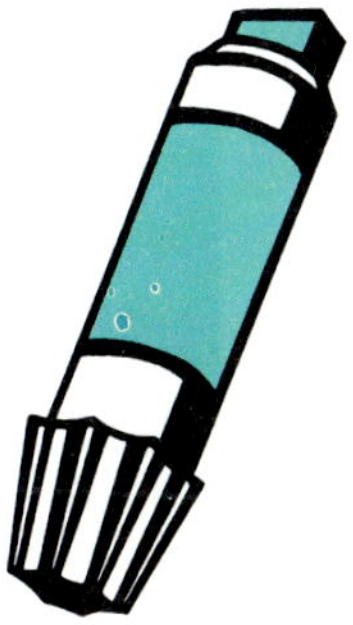

I. Spelling and Writing Read the story idea. Use the Spelling Words, Other Word Forms, and Challenge Words to help you think of an answer to each question. Proofread your work.

Story idea:
We heard a scream coming from the other room.

1. Who or what screamed?
2. What caused the scream?
3. Where did this take place?
4. When did this take place?
5. Who heard the scream?
6. What did the characters think about the situation?

35

A. Pretest and Proofreading

B. Spelling Words and Phrases

1.	omit	if you omit two words
2.	only	the only one left
3.	ocean	swam in the ocean
4.	opening	through the opening
5.	poem	a twelve-line poem
6.	hotel	staying at the hotel
7.	clothes	changed my clothes
8.	clothing	clothing store
9.	dash	fifty-yard dash
10.	ranch	a large ranch house
11.	branch	local branch of the library
12.	handy	the handy tool kit
13.	packed	packed too tightly
14.	package	package of gum
15.	landing	stepped onto the landing
16.	evening	a summer evening
17.	fever	a high fever
18.	everyone	enough for everyone
19.	everybody	if everybody knew
20.	everything	mixed everything together

Other Word Forms

omits, omitted, omitting
oceans
open, opens, opened, opener
poems, poet, poetry
hotels
cloth, clothe, clothed
dashes, dashed, dashing
rancher, ranches
branches, branched, branching
handier, handiest, handily
pack, packs, packing
packages, packaged
land, lands, landings
evenings
feverish

C. Visual Warm-up

Write each word in its correct shape.

a.

b.

c.

d.

e.

f.

g.

h.

i.

j.

k.

l.

m.

n.

o.

p.

q.

r.

s.

t.

D. Break the Code Use the code to write the spelling words.

a	b	c	d	e	f	g	h	i	j	k	l	m
↕	↕	↕	↕	↕	↕	↕	↕	↕	↕	↕	↕	↕
z	y	x	w	v	u	t	s	r	q	p	o	n

1. lxvzm ______
2. wzhs ______
3. kzxpztv ______
4. slgvo ______
5. xolgsrmt ______
6. lmob ______
7. lkvmrmt ______
8. uvevi ______
9. vevmrmt ______
10. ozmwrmt ______
11. veviblmv ______
12. klvn ______
13. xolgsvh ______
14. lnrg ______
15. vevibgsrmt ______
16. kzxpvw ______
17. szmwb ______
18. yizmxs ______
19. vevibylwb ______
20. izmxs ______

E. Word Search The spelling words can be found in the puzzle. The words appear across and down. Circle and write the words.

p	c	l	o	t	h	e	s	o	v	e
a	h	o	t	e	l	v	n	n	e	v
c	c	e	s	p	o	e	m	l	r	e
k	s	f	e	v	e	r	o	y	u	r
a	a	e	v	e	r	y	b	o	d	y
g	y	t	e	h	o	t	r	p	a	o
e	h	a	n	d	y	h	g	e	s	n
h	o	m	i	t	n	i	t	n	h	e
v	l	a	n	d	i	n	g	i	r	o
e	s	t	g	m	e	g	p	n	a	c
b	r	a	n	c	h	w	z	g	n	e
f	p	a	c	k	e	d	r	b	c	a
c	l	o	t	h	i	n	g	p	h	n

Across

1. ______
2. ______
3. ______
4. ______
5. ______
6. ______
7. ______
8. ______
9. ______
10. ______
11. ______

Down

12. ______
13. ______
14. ______
15. ______
16. ______
17. ______
18. ______
19. ______
20. ______

Spelling Words

omit	only	ocean	opening	poem
hotel	clothes	clothing	dash	ranch
branch	handy	packed	package	landing
evening	fever	everyone	everybody	everything

F. Sort Your Words

1. Sometimes *ing* is an ending added to a base word. Other times *ing* is part of the base word. Write the five spelling words that end in *ing*.

__________ __________ __________

__________ __________

Of the words you have just written, circle those in which *ing* is an ending added to a base word. If you need help, use the **Spelling Dictionary**.

2. Three spelling words end with the long *e* sound. Write them.

__________ __________ __________

What letter makes the long *e* sound? __________

3. Eight spelling words have a long *o* sound. Write them in alphabetical order.

a. __________ **d.** __________ **g.** __________

b. __________ **e.** __________ **h.** __________

c. __________ **f.** __________

4. Seven spelling words have a short *a* sound. Write them in alphabetical order.

a. __________ **d.** __________ **f.** __________

b. __________ **e.** __________ **g.** __________

c. __________

5. Two spelling words have not been used above. Write them.

__________ __________

G. Using Other Word Forms
Write the Other Word Form that fits each clue.

Base Words: open(er) handy(er) poem(t) ranch(er) omit(ed)

1. more handy ____________________
2. used to open things ____________________
3. writer of poems ____________________
4. cattle farmer ____________________
5. left out ____________________

H. Challenge Words
Write the Challenge Word that completes each sentence.

fractions	**confessed**	**stroke**	**sweeter**	**talented**

1. We arrived at the ____________________ of midnight.
2. Many actors are very ____________________ .
3. We learned to add whole numbers and ____________________ .
4. Your berries taste ____________________ than mine.
5. The suspect ____________________ to the crime.

I. Spelling and Writing
Write each set of words in a sentence. You may use Other Word Forms. Proofread your work.

1. landing – ocean
2. fever – evening
3. everyone – hotel
4. omit – package
5. only – poem
6. clothing – packed
7. clothes – ranch
8. opening – dash
9. everybody – branch
10. handy – everything
11. talented – fractions
12. confessed – sweeter
13. stroke – dashed

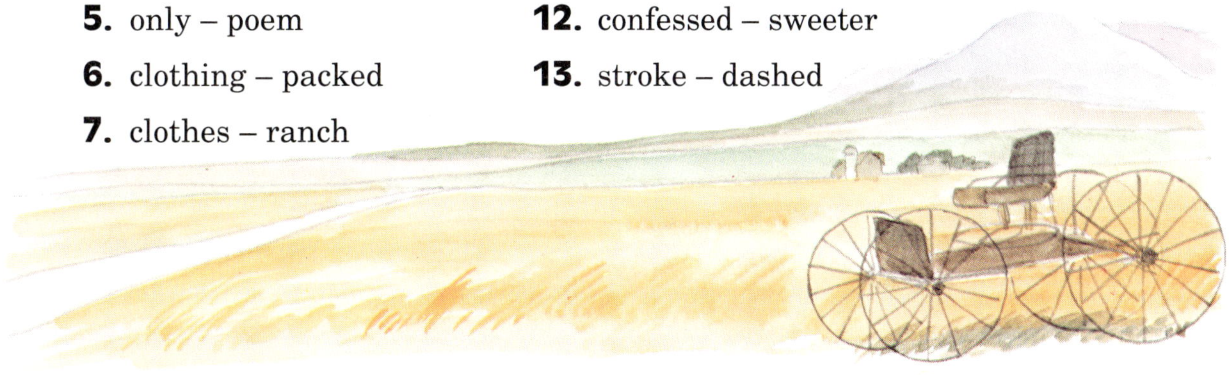

36 REVIEWING LESSONS 31-35

■	★	▲	◆	●
pool	playmate	sneakers	cable	ray
root	orange	picture	clothing	address
branch	sink	package	ocean	ranch
attic	baseball	fork	beat	tooth
pillow	stable	hotel	color	film

A. What Do You Need? Write Other Word Forms or the spelling words to complete the items. The shapes tell you in what column you can find the spelling word. Write each word or its Other Word Form only once. If you need help, use the **Spelling Dictionary**.

1. water in a swimming ■ __ __ __ __

2. friends or ★ __ __ __ __ __ __ __ __ __ to play tag

3. ◆ __ __ __ __ __ __ for trolley cars

4. the sun's ● __ __ __ __ to warm the earth

5. a ▲ __ __ __ __ __ __ __ with a shoelace that's not broken

6. fresh ★ __ __ __ __ __ __ __ to make juice

7. ◆ __ __ __ __ __ __ __ __ to wear to school

8. carrots with healthy ■ __ __ __ __ __

9. walls with ▲ __ __ __ __ __ __ __ __ hanging

10. numbers and streets for ● __ __ __ __ __ __ __ __ __ on letters

11. pretty paper and bows to wrap ▲ __ __ __ __ __ __ __ __

12. ovens, refrigerators, and ★ __ __ __ __ __ in kitchens

13. large farms or ● __ __ __ __ __ __ __ to raise animals

14. ■ __ __ __ __ __ __ __ __ on trees to climb

15. large ◆ __ __ __ __ __ __ for ships to sail

16. eggs that are ◆ __ __ __ __ __ __ to make breakfast

17. ● __ __ __ __ __ for chewing

18. bats and ★ __ __ __ __ __ __ __ __ __ to play a game

19. knives, ▲ __ __ __ __ __ , and spoons to eat a meal

20. ■ __ __ __ __ __ __ for storing old furniture

21. rooms in ▲ __ __ __ __ __ __ for travelers

22. ■ __ __ __ __ __ __ __ on a bed to lay your head

23. cameras for ● __ __ __ __ __ __ __ a movie

24. ◆ __ __ __ __ __ __ __ __ flags for the parade

25. clean ★ __ __ __ __ __ __ __ for horses

REVIEW

always	bigger	everything	July	middle
among	born	forty	June	October
another	enjoy	fourteen	leaving	only
anybody	everybody	fourth	May	since
before	everyone	gotten	means	sitting

B. Break the Code Use the code to write an Other Word Form or a spelling word. Write each word. Remember to use a capital letter for the calendar words.

a	b	c	d	e	f	g	h	i	j	k	l	m
↕	↕	↕	↕	↕	↕	↕	↕	↕	↕	↕	↕	↕
z	y	x	w	v	u	t	s	r	q	p	o	n

1. ovzevh
2. ylim
3. hrgh
4. qfmv
5. uligrvh
6. nrwwov
7. zmlgsvi
8. yvuliv
9. nzb
10. qfob
11. lmob
12. znlmthg
13. zodzbh
14. tvggrmt
15. ulfigvvmgs
16. vmqlbzyov
17. lxglyvi
18. hrmxv
19. veviblmv
20. yrttvhg
21. nvzmrmt
22. ulfigsh
23. vevibgsrmt
24. zmbylwb
25. vevibylwb

REVIEW

■	★	▲	◆	●
bloom	dream	huge	paste	sank
clothes	fever	kick	poem	speak
correct	flour	mouse	pound	steam
count	fort	omit	pretend	stream
dash	hour	packed	rich	woman

C. Word Clues Write the spelling word that goes with each clue. The shapes tell you in what column you can find the spelling word. Then write an Other Word Form for each spelling word. If you need help, use the **Spelling Dictionary**.

Word Clues	Spelling Words	Other Word Forms
1. a rhyming verse ◆	_ _ _ _	________
2. a sticky mixture ◆	_ _ _ _ _	________
3. to talk ●	_ _ _ _ _	________
4. seen while sleeping ★	_ _ _ _ _	________
5. went to the bottom ●	_ _ _ _	________
6. to make believe ◆	_ _ _ _ _ _ _	________
7. right ■	_ _ _ _ _ _ _	________
8. a blow with the foot ▲	_ _ _ _	________
9. a building ★	_ _ _ _	________
10. having a lot of money ◆	_ _ _ _	________
11. flowing water ●	_ _ _ _ _ _	________
12. 60 minutes ★	_ _ _ _	________
13. very large ▲	_ _ _ _	________
14. an adult female ●	_ _ _ _ _	________
15. a small furry animal ▲	_ _ _ _ _	________
16. to find the total ■	_ _ _ _ _	________
17. seen from a boiling kettle ●	_ _ _ _ _	________
18. to leave out ▲	_ _ _ _	________
19. a high temperature ★	_ _ _ _ _	________
20. a fast run ■	_ _ _ _	________
21. filled with items ▲	_ _ _ _ _ _	________
22. worn on the body ■	_ _ _ _ _ _ _	________
23. 16 ounces ◆	_ _ _ _ _	________
24. fine powder from grain ★	_ _ _ _ _	________
25. to flower ■	_ _ _ _ _	________

beast	follow	loop	pouring	second
corner	handy	nearest	reader	silk
evening	happening	opening	rules	single
fallen	inches	ounce	scream	waste
feast	landing	picnic	season	windy

D. Pack Your Suitcase Add, subtract, or do both to write Other Word Forms.

+ ed

1. pouring − ing + ed = ____________

2. happening − ing + ed = ____________

3. landing − ing + ed = ____________

4. rules − es + ed = ____________

5. inches − es + ed = ____________

6. opening − ing + ed = ____________

+ ing

7. reader − er + ing = ____________

8. fallen − en + ing = ____________

9. nearest − est + ing = ____________

+ est

10. silk + i + est = ____________

11. windy − y + i + est = ____________

12. handy − y + i + est = ____________

+ s

13. feast + s = ____________

14. loop + s = ____________

15. beast + s = ____________

16. waste + s = ____________

17. follow + s = ____________

18. season + s = ____________

19. second + s = ____________

20. corner + s = ____________

21. ounce + s = ____________

22. scream + s = ____________

23. single + s = ____________

24. picnic + s = ____________

25. evening + s = ____________

REVIEW

Spelling Dictionary/WORDFINDER

Your Spelling Dictionary/WORDFINDER lists all the basic spelling words and Other Word Forms in your spelling book. If the entry word is a spelling word, it is listed in **dark type**. If the entry word is not in dark type, then the spelling word is listed with the Other Word Forms at the end of the definition.

The Spelling Dictionary/WORDFINDER gives you a quick way to check the spelling and meanings of your spelling words. Because the Spelling Dictionary/WORDFINDER includes many of the words you will need in daily writing, you will find it useful for other schoolwork too.

Sample entries —

build |bĭld| *v.* To make something by putting together materials or parts: *to build a house.* ***builds, built, building, buildings, builder*** — Other Word Forms

built |bĭlt| *v.* Made something by putting together materials or parts: *built a bookcase.* [see *build*]

PRONUNCIATION KEY

ă	pat	j	judge	sh	dish, ship
ā	aid, fey, pay	k	cat, kick, pique	t	tight
â	air, care, wear	l	lid, needle	th	path, thin
ä	father	m	am, man, mum	*th*	bathe, this
b	bib	n	no, sudden	ŭ	cut, rough
ch	church	ng	thing	û	circle, firm, heard, term, turn, urge, word
d	deed	ŏ	horrible, pot	v	cave, valve, vine
ĕ	pet, pleasure	ō	go, hoarse, row, toe	w	with
ē	be, bee, easy, leisure	ô	alter, caught, for, paw	y	yes
f	fast, fife, off, phase, rough	oi	boy, noise, oil	yo͞o	abuse, use
g	gag	ou	cow, out	z	rose, size, xylophone, zebra
h	hat	o͝o	took	zh	garage, pleasure, vision
hw	which	o͞o	boot, fruit	ə	about, silent, pencil, lemon, circus
ĭ	pit	p	pop	ər	butter
ī	by, guy, pie	r	roar		
î	dear, deer, fierce, mere	s	miss, sauce, see		

STRESS

Primary stress ′ **bi•ol′o•gy** |bī ŏl′ə jē| Secondary stress ′ **bi′o•log′i•cal** |bī′ə lŏj′ĭ kəl|

A

above |ə bŭv′| *prep.* Over or higher than: *above the trees.*

absent |ăb′sənt| *adj.* Not present: *absent students.* ***absence, absently, absentee***

across |ə krôs′| *adv.* From one side to another: *across and over. prep.* To the other side of: *across the river.*

address |ə drĕs′| *n.* The place where a person lives or the place to which mail is sent: *his street address.* ***addresses, addressed, addressing***

afraid |ə frād′| *adj.* Feeling frightened or scared: *afraid to be alone.*

again |ə gĕn′| *adv.* One more time: *played the game again.*

agree |ə grē′| *v.* To think or feel the same way as another person: *will agree that bananas are yellow.* ***agrees, agreed, agreeing, agreeable, agreement***

ahead |ə hĕd′| *adv.* In front; farther forward: *will go ahead.*

aid |ād| *n.* Help or assistance: *thankful for their aid. v.* To help or give support to: *will aid the teacher.* ***aids, aided, aiding***

alike |ə līk′| *adv.* In the same way: *to walk alike. adj.* The same; similar: *to be alike in many ways.* ***alikeness***

almost |ôl′mōst| *adv.* Close to or nearly: *almost time to begin.* ***most, mostly***

alone |ə lōn′| *adj.* Without company; by oneself: *was alone in the dark.*

already |ôl rĕd′ē| *adv.* By a certain time: *already finished.*

always |ôl′ wāz| *adv.* At all times: *always sunny.*

among |ə mŭng′| *prep.* In the company of others: *among the animals in the zoo.* ***amongst***

amount |ə mount′| *n.* The total or sum: *amount of snow.* ***amounts, amounted, amounting***

another |ə nŭ*th*′ər| *pron.* One more or a different one: *asked for another.*

anybody |ĕn′ē bŏd′ē| *pron.* Any person: *if anybody can go.*

apiece |ə pēs′| *adv.* Each; for each one: *ten cents apiece.*

arithmetic |ə rĭth′mətĭk| *n.* Adding, subtracting, multiplying, and dividing: *mistake in my arithmetic.* ***arithmetical***

around |ə round′| *prep.* **1.** On the farther side of: *around the second bend.* **2.** In a circle about: *around the tree.*

attic |ăt′ĭk| *n.* The space just underneath the roof of a house: *stored in the attic.* ***attics***

awake |ə wāk′| *v.* To wake up: *will awake early.* ***awakes, awaked, awoke, awaking***

awoke |ə wōk′| *v.* Woke up: *awoke from a dream.* [see *awake*]

ax |ăks| *n.* A tool with a sharp blade, used for chopping wood: *the firefighter's ax.* ***axes, axed, axing***

B

backward |băk′wərd| *adj.* Moving toward the rear: *backward fall.* ***backwards***

banner |băn′ər| *n.* A flag: *a striped banner.* ***banners***

baseball |bās′bôl′| *adj.* Of or for baseball: *baseball mitt. n.* A game played with a ball and bat by two teams with nine players on a field with four bases: *new bat for baseball.* ***baseballs***

basket |băs′kĭt| *n.* A woven container: *a laundry basket.* ***baskets***

basketball |băs′kĭt bôl′| *n.* A game played on a court by two teams of five players who try to toss a ball through a basket open at the bottom: *plays basketball and tennis.* ***basketballs***

battle |băt′l| *n.* A fight: *an exciting battle.* ***battles, battled, battling, battler***

be |bē| *v.* To act in a certain way: *to be late.* ***am, is, are, was, were, being, been***

beast |bēst| *n.* A four-footed animal: *a wild beast.* ***beasts, beastly***

beat |bēt| *n.* A stroke, blow, or sound made again and again: *beat of the band.* ***beats, beaten, beating, beater***

beef |bēf| *adj.* Made of beef: *beef stew. n.* Meat from a cow, bull, or steer: *roast beef.* ***beefy***

before |bĭ fôr′| *conj.* Ahead of the time when: *before you arrive.*

began |bĭ găn′| *v.* Started: *began to run.* [see *begin*]

begin |bĭ gĭn′| *v.* To start: *will begin to rain.* ***begins, began, begun, beginning, beginner***

begun |bĭ gŭn′| *v.* Started: *since dinner has begun.* [see *begin*]

being |bē′ĭng| *v.* Acting in a certain way: *being very rude.* [see *be*]

belong |bĭ lông′| *v.* **1.** To have a proper place: *to belong here.* **2.** To be a member of: *does belong to the club.* ***belongs, belonged, belonging, belongings***

belonged |bĭ lôngd′| *v.* **1.** Had a proper place: *belonged in the cupboard.* **2.** Was a member of: *belonged to our group.* [see *belong*]

bend |bĕnd| *v.* To curve or make crooked: *will bend the metal. n.* A part that is not straight: *a bend in the wire.* ***bends, bent, bending, bendable***

between |bĭ twēn′| *prep.* In the space dividing two objects or places: *between the trees.*

bid |bĭd| *v.* To offer to pay or buy at a certain price: *will bid ten dollars.* ***bids, bidding, bidder***

big |bĭg| *adj.* Large; great in amount or size: *big mountain.* ***bigger, biggest***

bigger |bĭg′ər| *adj.* Larger; greater in amount or size: *a bigger piece of fruit.* [see *big*]

bind |bīnd| *v.* **1.** To fasten together between covers: *will bind these papers.* **2.** To fasten or tie together: *to bind with string or ribbon.* ***binds, bound, binding, binder***

birthday |bûrth′dā′| *n.* The day on which someone is born: *fourteenth birthday.* ***birthdays***

blade |blād| *n.* **1.** The metal part of an ice skate: *sharp blade on the new skate.* **2.** The flat, sharp part of an object used for cutting: *knife blade.* ***blades***

blame |blām| *n.* Responsibility, or duty, for something wrong: *took the blame. v.* To find fault: *will blame you for breaking the store window.* ***blames, blamed, blaming, blameful, blameless***

ă pat / ā pay / â care / ä father / ĕ pet / ē be / ĭ pit / ī pie / î fierce / ŏ pot / ō go / ô paw, for / oi oil / o͝o book / o͞o boot / ou out / ŭ cut / û fur / *th* the / th thin / hw which / zh vision / ə ago, item, pencil, atom, circus

blanket |blăng′kĭt| *n.* A woven covering used to keep people or animals warm: *a wool blanket.* ***blankets, blanketed, blanketing***

blast |blăst| *n.* An explosion, or loud noise: *a blast from the mine.* ***blasts, blasted, blasting***

blaze |blāz| *n.* A fire or a bright flame: *warmed by the blaze.* ***blazes, blazed, blazing***

blind |blīnd| *adj.* Hidden; hard to see: *blind curve.* ***blinds, blinded, blinding, blindly, blindness***

block |blŏk| *n.* Something hard and solid: *huge block of ice.* ***blocks, blocked, blocking, blocker***

blocks |blŏks| *n.* More than one block: *blocks of bricks.* [see *block*]

bloom |bloom| *v.* To have or open into flowers: *will bloom in April. n.* A flower or blossom: *a spring bloom.* ***blooms, bloomed, blooming, bloomer***

board |bôrd| *n.* A long, flat piece of wood used in building: *a four-foot board.* ***boards, boarded, boarding, boarder***

boil |boil| *v.* To bubble and give off steam due to heating: *will boil the soup.* ***boils, boiled, boiling, boiler***

born |bôrn| *adj.* Brought into life: *born on December 5.*

bother |bŏ*th*′ər| *v.* To trouble, annoy, or pester: *won't bother you with any noise.* ***bothers, bothered, bothering***

bound |bound| *v.* Fastened together; tied: *bound with rope.* [see *bind*]

branch |brănch| *n.* A division of a main part: *a branch of the road.* ***branches, branched, branching***

brave |brāv| *adj.* Not afraid: *the brave hero.* ***braver, bravest, braves, braved, braving, bravely, braveness, bravery***

break |brāk| *v.* To take or come apart: *to break a dish.* ***breaks, broke, broken, breaking, breaker***

breath |brĕth| *n.* The air that goes into and comes out of the lungs: *a deep breath.*—**Out of breath**—Breathless. ***breaths, breather, breathless, breathlessly, breathlessness, breathe, breathes, breathed, breathing***

brick |brĭk| *adj.* Made of bricks: *brick house. n.* A block of clay baked by sun or fire until hard: *built of brick.* ***bricks, bricked, bricking***

broke |brōk| *v.* Took or came apart: *broke the dish.* [see *break*]

bruise |brooz| *n.* An injury from a fall or blow that leaves a black-and-blue mark: *arm bruise.* ***bruises, bruised, bruising***

brush |brŭsh| *v.* To clean, sweep, groom, or paint with a brush: *to brush your hair.* ***brushes, brushed, brushing***

bucket |bŭk′it| *n.* A round container used for carrying such things as water, sand, milk, or coal: *a bucket of sand.* ***buckets***

build |bĭld| *v.* To make something by putting together materials or parts: *to build a house.* ***builds, built, building, buildings, builder***

built |bĭlt| *v.* Made something by putting together materials or parts: *built a bookcase.* [see *build*]

bump |bŭmp| *n.* **1.** A small place that rises above what is around it: *a bump in the road.* **2.** A lump or swelling: *bump on his head.* ***bumps, bumped, bumping, bumper, bumpy***

burn |bûrn| *v.* To set on fire: *to burn the pile of leaves.* *n.* An injury caused by fire or heat: *a burn from the hot pan.* ***burns, burned, burnt, burning, burner***

busy |**bĭz**′e| *adj.* Active; working; having plenty to do: *busy person.* ***busier, busiest, busyness***

C

cabin |**kăb**′ĭn| *n.* A small, plain house: *cabin made of logs.* ***cabins***

cable |**kā**′bəl| *n.* A strong, thick rope made of twisted wire: *to pull the heavy wagon with a cable.*—**Cable car**—A car pulled by an overhead or undergound cable. ***cables, cabled***

camel |**kăm**′ əl| *n.* A large four-footed animal with either one or two humps and a long neck, found in Africa and Asia: *a camel at the zoo.* ***camels***

candle |**kăn**′dl| *n.* A stick of wax with a wick inside: *tall, thin candle.* ***candles***

can't |kănt| Contraction for *cannot: can't go home.*

cape |kāp| *n.* A sleeveless coat that hangs loosely from the shoulders, fastened at the neck: *a winter cape.* ***capes***

care |kâr| *n.* Attention or caution: *to iron the clothes with care.* ***cares, cared, caring, careless, carelessly, carelessness, careful, carefully, carefulness***

careful |**kâr**′fəl| *adj.* Paying attention; cautious: *a careful driver.* [see *care*]

careless |**kâr**′lis| *adj.* Not paying attention: *was careless and fell.* [see *care*]

case |kās| *n.* A container to hold something: *a leather case.* ***cases, cased, casing***

cases |**kā**′sĭz| *n.* More than one case: *wooden cases for toys.* [see *case*]

cash |kăsh| *v.* To get money for: *to cash a check.* *n.* Money in the form of bills and coins: *extra cash in the bank.* ***cashes, cashed, cashing, cashier***

cattle |**kăt**′l| *n.* Cows, bulls, and steers raised for meat and milk: *herd of cattle.*

cent |sĕnt| *n.* A penny; a coin of the United States and Canada: *one cent.* ***cents***

center |**sĕn**′tər| *n.* The middle part or place of something: *in the center of the table.* ***centers, centered, centering, central***

cents |sĕnts| *n.* More than one penny: *two cents.* [see *cent*]

chain |chān| *n.* A row of rings joined together: *a gold chain.* ***chains, chained, chaining***

chance |chăns| *n.* The possibility that something will happen: *a good chance of rain.* ***chances, chanced, chancing***

change |chānj| *n.* **1.** A passing from one form or place to another: *a change of weather.* **2.** Money given back when a larger amount is paid than the price of what is bought: *ten cents in change.* *v.* To put something in place of another: *will change the sheets.* ***changes, changed, changing, changeable***

chart |chärt| *n.* A table, diagram, graph, etc., that gives information: *a weather chart.* ***charts, charted, charting***

ă pat / ā pay / â care / ä father / ĕ pet / ē be / ĭ pit / ī pie / î fierce / ŏ pot / ō go / ô paw, for / oi oil / o͝o book / o͞o boot / ou out / ŭ cut / û fur / *th* the / th thin / hw which / zh vision / ə ago, item, pencil, atom, circus

chase |chās| *n.* The act of following after and trying to catch: *a long chase. v.* To follow in order to catch: *to chase them through the woods.* ***chases, chased, chasing, chaser***

check |chĕk| *n.* A written order telling a bank to pay money to the person named: *paid by check.* ***checks, checked, checking, checker***

cheer |chîr| *v.* **1.** To give a shout of happiness, support, or praise: *to cheer loudly at the game.* **2.** To make or become happier: *a gift to cheer you.* ***cheers, cheered, cheering, cheerful, cheerfully, cheery, cheerier, cheeriest, cheeriness***

choose |chōōz| *v.* To pick from a group: *will choose another seat.* ***chooses, chose, chosen, choosing, choosy, choosier, choosiest, choosiness, chooser***

chop |chŏp| *n.* A small piece of meat with a bone: *a pork chop. v.* To cut by hitting with a sharp tool: *will chop the carrots for dinner.* ***chops, chopped, chopping, chopper***

chose |chōz| *v.* Picked from a group: *chose a book.* [see *choose*]

clever |klĕv′ər| *adj.* Showing quick thinking; skillful: *clever idea.* ***cleverer, cleverest, cleverly, cleverness***

climb |klīm| *v.* To move upward using hands and feet: *can climb a tree like a monkey.* ***climbs, climbed, climbing, climber***

cloth |klôth| *n.* A piece of woven material used in making clothes: *cotton cloth.* ***cloths, clothe, clothes, clothed, clothing***

clothes |klōz| *n.* Things worn to cover the body: *bought new clothes.* [see *cloth*]

clothing |klō′thĭng| *adj.* Of or for clothing: *clothing brush. n.* Clothes: *warm winter clothing.* [see *cloth*]

clown |kloun| *n.* A person who makes people laugh: *a circus clown.* ***clowns, clowned, clowning, clownish***

club |klŭb| *adj.* Of a club: *club trip. n.* A group of people meeting for a special purpose: *a club at school.* ***clubs, clubbed, clubbing***

coach |kōch| *n.* A teacher or trainer of athletes and performers: *our team's coach.* ***coaches, coached, coaching***

coal |kōl| *n.* A black mineral used for fuel: *heats with coal.* ***coals***

coin |koin| *n.* A flat, round piece of metal used as money: *a silver coin.* ***coins, coined, coining, coinage***

color |kŭl′ər| *n.* One of the parts of the spectrum; a certain shade, hue, or tint: *a bright color in the painting.* ***colors, colored, coloring, colorful***

copy |kŏp′ē| *v.* To make something exactly like something else: *will copy this word. n.* Something made to look exactly like something else: *made a copy of the letter.* ***copies, copied, copying, copier***

corner |kôr′nər| *n.* The place where two surfaces or lines meet: *corner of the room.* ***corners, cornered, cornering***

correct |kə rĕkt′| *adj.* Right; not having mistakes: *correct answer. v.* To mark the mistakes in: *will correct the test.* ***corrects, corrected, correcting, correctly, correction, correctness***

count |kount| *v.* To find the total number of: *to count correctly.* ***counts, counted, counting, counter***

crack |krăk| *n.* A narrow split or opening: *crack in the earth.* ***cracks, cracked, cracking, cracker***

crash |krăsh| *v.* To fall, hit, or break suddenly with a loud noise: *will crash into the table. n.* A forceful fall, hit, or break with a loud noise: *the crash of dishes.* ***crashes, crashed, crashing***

cried |krīd| *v.* Shed tears: *cried all night.* [see *cry*]

crime |krīm| *n.* An action against the law: *the crime of stealing.* **crimes, criminal**

cross |krôs| *v.* To draw a line across: *will cross a* t. ***crosses, crossed, crossing***

crossing |**krô**′sĭng| *v.* Drawing a line across: *crossing out mistakes.* [see *cross*]

crowd |kroud| *n.* A large number of people gathered together: *a crowd of students.* ***crowds, crowded, crowding***

cry |krī| *v.* To shed tears: *to cry when sad.* ***cries, cried, crying, crier***

D

dance |dăns| *v.* To move in time to music: *likes to dance fast.* ***dances, danced, dancing, dancer***

dancing |**dăn**′sĭng| *v.* Moving in time to music: *dancing the waltz.* [see *dance*]

danger |**dān**′jər| *n.* The chance of something bad happening: *was full of danger.* ***dangers, dangerous, dangerously***

dare |dâr| *v.* To have courage to try: *to dare to escape. n.* A challenge or contest: *a dare to jump.* ***dares, dared, daring, daringly***

dash |dăsh| *n.* A fast run: *a dash for the door.* ***dashes, dashed, dashing***

dawn |dôn| *n.* Daybreak; the time at which daylight first appears: *left before dawn.* ***dawns, dawned, dawning***

death |dĕth| *n.* The end of living: *the bird's death.* ***deaths, deathly***

December |dĭ **sĕm**′bər| *adj.* Of December: *December storm. n.* The last and twelfth month in the year: *the first week of December.* ***Dec.***

deck |dĕk| *n.* **1.** A level on a ship: *the lower deck.* **2.** A set of playing cards: *shuffled the deck.* ***decks, decked, decking***

deliver |dĭ **lĭv**′ər| *v.* To carry and hand out: *to deliver the mail.* ***delivers, delivered, delivering, delivery, deliverer***

demand |dĭ **mănd**′| *v.* To ask for strongly: *to demand an answer.* ***demands, demanded, demanding***

didn't |**dĭd**′nt| Contraction for *did not: didn't finish.*

dim |dĭm| *v.* To make less bright: *to dim the headlights. adj.* Having or giving little light; not bright: *dim moonlight.* ***dims, dimmed, dimming, dimmer, dimmest, dimly, dimness***

dirt |dûrt| *n.* Dust, mud, or any material that makes something unclean: *dirt on his face.* ***dirty, dirtier, dirtiest, dirties, dirtied, dirtying***

dirty |**dûr**′tē| *adj.* Unclean: *dirty hands.* [see *dirt*]

discover |dĭ **skŭv**′ər| *v.* To find out for the first time: *might discover buried treasure.* ***discovers, discovered, discovering, discoverer, discovery***

ă pat / ā pay / â care / ä father / ĕ pet / ē be / ĭ pit / ī pie / î fierce / ŏ pot / ō go / ô paw, for / oi oil / o͝o book / o͞o boot / ou out / ŭ cut / û fur / *th* the / th thin / hw which / zh vision / ə ago, item, pencil, atom, circus

dive |dīv| *n.* A headfirst plunge into water: *a dive into the pool.* ***dives, dived, dove, diving, diver***

draft |drăft| *n.* A flow of air: *a cold draft from the broken window.* ***drafts, drafted, drafting***

drag |drăg| *v.* To pull or move slowly and heavily: *to drag the heavy box.* ***drags, dragged, dragging, dragger***

drain |drān| *v.* To draw off or flow off slowly: *will drain the liquid. n.* A pipe for carrying off water or waste: *a drain for the bathroom sink.* ***drains, drained, draining***

drank |drăngk| *v.* Swallowed liquids: *drank a glass of milk.* [see *drink*]

draw |drô| *v.* To pull or take out: *to draw a winning number from the hat.* ***draws, drew, drawn, drawing, drawings, drawer***

dream |drēm| *n.* The pictures and thoughts seen during sleep: *had a scary dream about monsters.* ***dreams, dreamed, dreamt, dreaming, dreamy, dreamer***

drill |drĭl| *n.* A tool for making holes in hard material: *the electric drill.* ***drills, drilled, drilling***

drink |drĭngk| *v.* To swallow liquids: *to drink slowly.* ***drinks, drank, drunk, drinking***

drive |drīv| *v.* To control the movement of a car or other vehicle: *to drive to the store for groceries.* ***drives, drove, driving, driver***

driving |**drī**′vĭng| *v.* Controlling the movement of a car or other vehicle: *was driving a truck.* [see *drive*]

during |**dŏŏr**′ĭng| *prep.* **1.** Through the entire time of: *during the storm.* **2.** At some point of time: *during the first hour.*

E

early |**ûr**′lē| *adv.* At or close to the beginning of a time period: *woke early in the morning.* ***earlier, earliest***

earn |ûrn| *v.* To get paid for work done: *to earn twenty dollars.* ***earns, earned, earning, earnings, earner***

earth |ûrth| *n.* The planet we live on: *circled the earth.* ***earthy, earthen, earthly***

eleven |ĭ **lĕv**′ən| *n.* A number equal to one more than ten; *eleven plus two.* ***elevens, eleventh***

enjoy |ĕn **joi**′| *v.* To be happy with; get joy and pleasure from: *to enjoy downhill skiing.* ***enjoys, enjoyed, enjoying, enjoyable, enjoyably, enjoyment***

enter |**ĕn**′tər| *v.* **1.** To join; become a member of: *will enter the contest.* **2.** To go or come into: *to enter the room.* ***enters, entered, entering, entrance***

evening |**ēv**′nĭng| *n.* The time between late afternoon and early nighttime: *five o'clock in the evening.* ***evenings***

event |ĭ **vĕnt**′| *n.* One of the contests in a program of sports: *the final event.* ***events, eventful, eventfully***

everybody |**ĕv**′rē bŏd′ē| *pron.* All people: *everybody here.*

everyone |**ĕv**′rē wŭn′| *pron.* Everybody: *everyone in the room.*

everything |**ĕv**′rē thĭng′| *pron.* All things; *everything you bought.*

F

fade |fād| *v.* To dim; lose color: *will fade in the sun.* ***fades, faded, fading***

fall |fôl| *v.* To drop from a higher place: *to fall from a ladder.* ***falls, fell, falling, fallen***

fallen |fô′lən| *adj.* Down on the ground: *fallen leaves.* [see *fall*]

far |fär| *adv.* To or at a great distance: *far from home.* ***farther, farthest***

farther |fär′*th*ər| *adv.* To or at a greater distance: *farther from shore.* [see *far*]

fate |fāt| *n.* **1.** What happens to a person or thing: *the fate of snow on a warm day.* **2.** The power believed to control what will happen: *caused by fate.* ***fates, fated, fateful***

fear |fîr| *v.* To feel afraid or that danger pain, or the unknown is near: *does fear the dark.* ***fears, feared, fearing, fearful, fearfully, fearfulness, fearless, fearlessly, fearlessness***

fears |fîrz| *v.* Feels afraid or that danger, pain, or the unknown is near: *fears large animals.* [see *fear*]

feast |fēst| *n.* A large meal prepared for a special occasion: *cooked for the king's feast.* ***feasts, feasted, feasting***

February |fĕb′ro͞o ĕr′ē| *n.* The second month in the year: *not until February.* ***Feb.***

feel |fēl| *v.* To have the sense of being: *to feel sad.* ***feels, felt, feeling, feelings, feeler***

feeling |fē′lĭng| *v.* Having the sense of being: *feeling warm.* [see *feel*]

fence |fĕns| *n.* A railing or wall used to protect or mark off an area: *a wooden fence around the yard.* ***fences, fenced, fencing, fencer***

fever |fē′vər| *n.* A body temperature higher than usual: *sick with a fever.* ***fevers, feverish***

few |fyo͞o| *adj.* Not many: *a few people.* ***fewer, fewest***

field |fēld| *n.* An open land with few or no trees: *ran across the field behind the school.* ***fields***

film |fĭlm| *n.* A motion picture; movie: *went to see the new film.* ***films, filmed, filming, filmy***

fireplace |fîr′plās′| *n.* An opening in a room for holding a fire: *burned in the fireplace.* ***fireplaces***

flash |flăsh| *n.* **1.** A sudden, short blast of light: *a flash of lightning.* **2.** An instant; a split second: *happened in a flash.* ***flashes, flashed, flashing, flasher, flashy***

fled |flĕd| *v.* Ran away from: *fled the fire.* [see *flee*]

flee |flē| *v.* To run away from: *to flee danger.* ***flees, fled, fleeing***

flock |flŏk| *n.* A group of one kind of animal: *a flock of geese.* ***flocks, flocked, flocking***

floor |flôr| *n.* **1.** The part of a room that a person stands or walks on: *a wooden floor.* **2.** A level, or story, of a building: *lives on the second floor.* ***floors***

flour |flour| *n.* A fine powder made by grinding grains: *measured flour for the vanilla cake.* ***flours, floured, flouring, floury***

flow |flō| *n.* Any steady, smooth movement: *the flow of the water.* ***flows, flowed, flowing***

ă pat / ā pay / â care / ä father / ĕ pet / ē be / ĭ pit / ī pie / î fierce / ŏ pot / ō go / ô paw, for / oi oil / o͝o book / o͞o boot / ou out / ŭ cut / û fur / *th* the / th thin / hw which / zh vision / ə ago, item, pencil, atom, circus

follow |fŏl′ō| *v.* To go or come after: *to follow the leader.* ***follows, followed, following, follower***

fond |fŏnd| *adj.* Loving or liking: *a fond hug.* **—Fond of—**Having a liking for. ***fonder, fondest, fondly, fondness***

fork |fôrk| *n.* **1.** One of the parts into which something divides: *the left fork in the road.* **2.** An eating tool with a handle at one end and pointed parts at the other: *a fork and a spoon.* ***forks, forked, forking***

fort |fôrt| *n.* A building or area that soldiers protect against an enemy: *the army's fort.* ***forts, fortress, fortify***

forty |fôr′tē| *adj.* Four times ten: *forty pennies.* ***forties, fortieth***

four |fôr| *adj.* One more than three: *four oranges.* ***fours, fourth, fourths***

fourteen |fôr′tēn′| *adj.* Four more than ten: *fourteen students.* ***fourteens, fourteenth***

fourth |fôrth| *adj.* Next after the third: *fourth grade.* [see *four*]

frame |frām| *n.* A form that borders something: *the window frame.* ***frames, framed, framing, framer***

freeze |frēz| *v.* To harden into a solid by cold: *to freeze water into ice.* ***freezes, froze, frozen, freezing, freezer***

fresh |frĕsh| *adj.* Just made or grown: *fresh bread.* ***fresher, freshest, freshly, freshness***

Friday |frī′dā′| *adj.* Of Friday: *Friday cookout. n.* The sixth day of the week: *every Friday.* ***Fri.***

fried |frīd| *adj.* Cooked in fat: *a pan of fried potatoes.* [see *fry*]

friend |frĕnd| *n.* A person someone knows and likes: *my good friend.* ***friends, friendly, friendlier, friendliest***

friends |frĕndz| *n.* More than one friend: *his friends at school.* [see *friend*]

front |frŭnt| *adj.* At or near the forward part: *on the front page. n.* The part that comes first or faces forward: *the front of the room.* ***fronts***

froze |frōz| *v.* Became hardened by cold: *when the pond froze.* [see *freeze*]

fry |frī| *v.* To cook in fat: *to fry eggs.* ***fries, fried, frying, fryer***

G

gang |găng| *n.* A group of people who work or play together: *a gang of friends. v.* To form into a group: *to gang together for the trip.* **—Gang up on—**To attack as a group. ***gangs, ganged, ganging***

get |gĕt| *v.* To be or become: *to get warmer.* ***gets, got, gotten, getting***

glass |glăs| *n.* A hard material that breaks easily and can be seen through: *broken glass.* ***glasses, glassy, glassful***

glasses |glăs′ĭz| *n.* A pair of glass lenses worn to help a person see better: *glasses with gold frames.* [see *glass*]

globe |glōb| *n.* A world map in the shape of a ball: *the globe in our classroom.* ***globes, global***

glow |glō| *n.* A light made by a fire, star, electricity, etc.: *the glow from the bulb.* ***glows, glowed, glowing***

gold |gōld| *n.* A bright-yellow color: *red, blue, and gold.* ***golds, golden***

golden |gōl′dən| *adj.* Bright-yellow: *long golden hair.* [see *gold*]

gotten |gŏt′n| *v.* Become: *had gotten tired.* [see *get*]

gown |goun| *n.* A long dress: *a new gown for the party.* ***gowns***

grandmother |grănd′mŭth′ər| *n.* The mother of one's father or mother: *visited my grandmother.* ***grandmothers***

greet |grēt| *v.* To welcome in a friendly way: *to greet the guests.* ***greets, greeted, greeting, greeter***

grind |grīnd| *v.* To crush into small pieces or powder: *to grind into flour.* ***grinds, ground, grinding, grinder***

grip |grĭp| *n.* A tight hold or grasp: *a grip on the rope.* ***grips, gripped, gripping***

grow |grō| *v.* **1.** To become: *to grow dark.* **2.** To cause to become bigger; raise: *to grow vegetables.* ***grows, grew, grown, growing, growth***

grown |grōn| *v.* **1.** Become: *had grown very tall.* **2.** Caused to become bigger; raised: *had grown corn.* [see *grow*]

H

habit |hăb′ĭt| *n.* An action repeated over and over: *a habit of going to sleep early.* ***habits***

hammer |hăm′ər| *n.* A tool with a metal head at the end of a long handle, used for driving nails: *a hammer and a saw.* ***hammers, hammered, hammering***

handle |hăn′dl| *n.* The part of an object that is grasped or held by the hand: *the handle of the shovel.* ***handles, handled, handling, handler***

handy |hăn′dē| *adj.* Easy to reach: *the handy bookshelf.* ***handier, handiest, handily, handiness***

hang |hăng| *v.* To fasten to something above: *to hang your coat on the hook.* ***hangs, hanged, hung, hanging, hanger***

happen |hăp′ən| *v.* To take place; occur: *to happen to us.* ***happens, happened, happening***

happening |hăp′ə nĭng| *v.* Taking place; occurring: *happening tomorrow night.* [see *happen*]

harm |härm| *n.* Damage or injury: *caused harm to the forests.* *v.* To cause damage or injury to; hurt: *could harm you.* ***harms, harmed, harming, harmful, harmless, harmlessness***

hate |hāt| *v.* To dislike very much: *to hate spiders.* ***hates, hated, hating, hateful, hatefully***

hear |hîr| *v.* To take in sounds through the ear: *to hear the loud music.* ***hears, heard, hearing***

heard |hûrd| *v.* Took in sounds through the ear: *heard the dog barking.* [see *hear*]

heart |härt| *n.* A red shape with rounded sides meeting in a point at the bottom and forming two curves at the top: *drew a red heart.* ***hearts, hearty, heartier, heartiest***

heat |hēt| *v.* To make or become warm: *will heat our dinner.* ***heats, heated, heating, heater***

heating |hē′tĭng| *v.* Making or becoming warm: *heating the milk.* [see *heat*]

heel |hēl| *n.* The piece of a shoe or boot under the back part of the foot: *a new heel for the shoe.* ***heels, heeled, heeling***

ă pat / ā pay / â care / ä father / ĕ pet / ē be / ĭ pit / ī pie / î fierce / ŏ pot / ō go / ô paw, for / oi oil / o͝o book / o͞o boot / ou out / ŭ cut / û fur / *th* the / th thin / hw which / zh vision / ə ago, item, pencil, atom, circus

hero |hîr′ō| *n.* A person noted and admired for courage, bravery, etc.: *a hero in battle.* ***heroes, heroic, heroism***

he's |hēz| Contraction for *he is: if he's waiting.*

high |hī| *adj.* Tall: *a high mountain.* ***higher, highest, highly, highness***

higher |hī′ər| *adj.* Taller: *higher kite.* [see *high*]

highest |hī′ĭst| *adj.* Tallest: *the highest building.* [see *high*]

highway |hī′wā′| *n.* A main road: *a two-lane highway.* ***highways***

hire |hīr| *v.* To pay for work: *will hire two painters.* ***hires, hired, hiring***

history |hĭs′tə rē| *n.* A record of past events: *the history of Europe. adj.* Of history: *a history test.* ***histories, historic, historical, historian***

hold |hōld| *v.* To take and keep in one's hands: *to hold the books.* **—Hold off—**To delay or wait. ***holds, held, holding, holdings, holder***

holding |hōl′dĭng| *v.* Taking and keeping in one's hands: *holding two packages.* [see *hold*]

hole |hōl| *n.* **1.** An opening: *hole in my shirt.* **2.** A hollow place in something solid: *dug a hole.* ***holes, holey***

holes |hōlz| *n.* **1.** Openings: *holes in the cloth.* **2.** Hollow places: *two holes in the wall.* [see *hole*]

homesick |hōm′sĭk′| *adj.* Sad because of being away from home: *a homesick traveler.* ***homesickness***

honey |hŭn′ē| *n.* A sweet liquid made by bees: *a spoonful of honey.* ***honeys, honeyed***

hope |hōp| *v.* To wish: *does hope to get a new sweater.* ***hopes, hoped, hoping, hopeful, hopefully, hopefulness, hopeless, hopelessly, hopelessness***

hoping |hō′pĭng| *v.* Wishing: *hoping to win.* [see *hope*]

hotel |hō tĕl′| *n.* A building that provides rooms and food for pay: *a room at the hotel.* ***hotels***

hour |our| *n.* A period of time equal to 60 minutes: *waited for an hour.* ***hours, hourly, hr.***

huge |hyo͞oj| *adj.* Very big: *a huge canyon.* ***huger, hugest, hugely, hugeness***

hundred |hŭn′drĭd| *n.* Ten times ten: *one hundred.* ***hundreds, hundreth***

hung |hŭng| *v.* Fastened to something above: *hung my coat.* [see *hang*]

hunger |hŭng′gər| *n.* The desire, or want, for food: *a hunger for vegetables.* ***hungers, hungered, hungering, hungry, hungrier, hungriest, hungrily, hungriness***

hungry |hŭng′grē| *adj.* Desiring, or wanting, food: *was not very hungry.* [see *hunger*]

hunt |hŭnt| *v.* To search or look for: *to hunt buried treasure.* ***hunts, hunted, hunting, hunter, hunters***

hunter |hŭn′tər| *n.* A person who hunts or searches for something: *a hunter in the hills.* [see *hunt*]

I

inch |ĭnch| *n.* A measure of length equal to one twelfth of a foot: *one inch of snow.* ***inches, inched, inching, inching, in.***

inches |ĭnch′ĭz| *n.* More than one inch: *sixty inches tall.* [see *inch*]

indeed |ĭn dēd′| *adv.* In fact; really; truly: *is indeed pleased.*

iron |ī′ərn| *v.* To press clothes with a heated iron: *to iron the shirt. n.* A household tool with a flat bottom which is heated and used to press clothes: *unplugged the iron.* ***irons, ironed, ironing***

island |ī′lənd| *n.* A piece of land surrounded by water: *sailed to the island.* ***islands, islander***

it's |ĭts| Contraction for *it is: since it's cold outside.*

itself |ĭt sĕlf′| *pron.* A form used in place of *it,* often to show importance: *the monkey itself.*

J

jail |jāl| *n.* A building where people who have broken the law are kept: *the county jail.* ***jails, jailed, jailing, jailer***

January |jăn′yoo͞ ĕr′ē| *adj.* Of January: *a January vacation. n.* The first month in the year: *a birthday in January.* ***Jan.***

jar |jär| *n.* A glass or clay container with a wide mouth: *a jar of jelly.* ***jars, jarred, jarring***

job |jŏb| *n.* Work that has to be done: *his job to wash the dishes.* ***jobs***

join |join| *v.* To meet: *to join our friends.* ***joins, joined, joining, joiner***

July |joo͞ lī′| *n.* The seventh month in the year: *going swimming in July.*

June |joo͞n| *n.* The sixth month in the year: *the last day in June.*

K

keep |kēp| *v.* **1.** To continue in a certain place or condition: *to keep together.* **2.** To have or hold for a long time: *will keep this picture.* ***keeps, kept, keeping, keeper***

kept |kĕpt| *v.* **1.** Continued in a certain place or condition: *kept quiet.* **2.** Had or held for a long time: *kept the ring in a safe place.* [see *keep*]

kick |kĭk| *n.* A blow with the foot: *a swift kick. v.* To move something by striking with the foot, or kicking: *will kick the ball.* ***kicks, kicked, kicking, kicker***

knee |nē| *n.* The joint where the thigh and lower leg meet: *fell on my knee.* ***knees, kneel, kneels, knelt, kneeled, kneeling***

knew |noo͞| *v.* **1.** Skilled in: *knew how to type.* **2.** Was sure of the facts: *knew the answer.* [see *know*]

knife |nīf| *n.* A sharp tool used for cutting: *sliced with a knife.* ***knifes, knifed, knifing, knives***

knot |nŏt| *n.* A fastening made by tying together pieces of rope or string: *a knot in my shoelace.* ***knots, knotted, knotting, knotty***

know |nō| *v.* **1.** To have skill in: *to know how to dance.* **2.** To be sure of the facts: *to know the exact date.* ***knows, knew, known, knowing, knowingly, knowledge***

knows |nōz| *v.* **1.** Has skill in: *knows how to sing.* **2.** Is sure of the facts: *knows where you live.* [see *know*]

ă **pat** / ā **pay** / â **care** / ä **father** / ĕ **pet** / ē **be** / ĭ **pit** / ī **pie** / î **fierce** / ŏ **pot** / ō **go** / ô **paw, for** / oi **oil** / o͝o **book** / o͞o **boot** / ou **out** / ŭ **cut** / û **fur** / *th* **the** / th **thin** / hw **which** / zh **vision** / ə **ago, item, pencil, atom, circus**

L

lace |lās| *adj.* Made of lace: *lace curtains. n.* Fine threads woven in an open pattern: *trimmed with lace. v.* To fasten or tie with a string: *will lace my shoes.* ***laces, laced, lacing, lacy***

ladder |**lăd**′ər| *n.* A piece of equipment used for climbing: *up the ladder.* ***ladders***

lamb |lăm| *n.* A young sheep: *a sleeping lamb.* ***lambs***

land |lănd| *n.* The surface of the earth not covered by water: *saw land from afar.* ***lands, landed, landing, landings***

landing |**lăn**′dĭng| *n.* **1.** The platform between a set of stairs: *stopped on the landing.* **2.** A wharf or pier: *swam to the landing.* [see *land*]

late |lāt| *adv.* After the proper time: *arrived late.* ***lately, later, latest, lateness***

lately |**lāt**′lē| *adv.* Not long ago: *have seen him lately.* [see *late*]

laugh |lăf| *v.* To make sounds that show happiness or enjoyment: *to laugh at the clown.* ***laughs, laughed, laughing, laughable, laughter***

law |lô| *n.* A rule that must be followed: *obeys the law.* ***laws, lawful, lawless, lawyer***

lawn |lôn| *n.* An area of grass around a house or building: *will mow the front lawn.* **—Lawn mower—**A machine for cutting grass. ***lawns***

laws |lôz| *n.* More than one law: *broke no laws.* [see *law*]

lazy |**lā**′zē| *adj.* Not want to work or be active: *am lazy in the summer.* ***lazier, laziest, lazily, laziness***

lead |lēd| *v.* To go to or be at the head of: *to lead the band.* ***leads, led, leading, leader***

leading |**lē**′dĭng| *v.* Going to or being at the head of: *leading the race.* [see *lead*]

leaf |lēf| *n.* One of the thin, flat parts of a plant: *a leaf on the tree.* ***leaves, leafy***

leak |lēk| *n.* A hole that lets something in or out by accident: *the tire with the leak.* ***leaks, leaked, leaking, leaky***

lean |lēn| *v.* To rest on a person or thing for support: *to lean against the wall.* ***leans, leaned, leaning, leaner, leanest***

leave |lēv| *v.* To go away: *to leave at noon.* ***leaves, left, leaving***

leaving |**lē**′vĭng| *v.* Going away: *leaving tomorrow.* [see *leave*]

led |lĕd| *v.* Showed or guided: *led the flock of sheep.* [see *lead*]

lend |lĕnd| *v.* To let someone have or use for a time: *will lend you a sweater.* ***lends, lent, lending, lender***

less |lĕs| *pron.* Fewer things or people: *has less than you do. adj.* Not a large amount of: *have less homework.* **—Much less—** Especially not. [see *little*]

lesson |**lĕs**′ən| *n.* Something that is learned or taught: *a spelling lesson.* ***lessons***

let |lĕt| *v.* To allow: *to let him go.* ***lets, letting***

letting |**lĕt**′ĭng| *v.* Allowing: *letting him speak.* [see *let*]

level |**lĕv**əl| *adj.* At an equal height: *level with the dining table.* ***levels, leveled, leveling, levelness***

lie |lī| *v.* To tell something that is not true: *to lie about where you went.* ***lies, lied, lying, liar***

light |līt| *adj.* Having little weight; not heavy: *a light box.* ***lights, lighted, lit, lighting, lightly, lighter, lightest, lightness***

lightly |lītʹlē| *adv.* With little force or weight; softly: *floating lightly on air.* [see *light*]

lightning |lītʹnĭng| *n.* A bright flash of light in the sky: *thunder and lightning.*

like |līk| *v.* To be pleased with: *to like our new neighbors.* ***likes, liked, liking, likely, likelier, likeliest, likeness***

likely |līkʹlē| *adj.* To be expected: *likely to be cold.* [see *like*]

little |lĭtʹl| *adj.* Small; not big or large; not much: *little time to talk.* ***littler, littlest, less, lesser, least, lessen, lessens, lessened, lessening***

live |lĭv| *v.* To make a home: *to live on Main Street.* ***lives, lived, living***

living |lĭvʹĭng| *v.* Making a home: *living in the city.* [see *live*]

load |lōd| *n.* A thing to carry: *a load of sand.* ***loads, loaded, loading, loader***

loads |lōdz| *n.* More than one load: *two loads of hay.* [see *load*]

lock |lŏk| *v.* To close with a lock: *will lock the front door.* ***unlock, unlocks, unlocked, unlocking***

loop |lo͞op| *n.* The rounded shape formed when a piece of rope or string crosses itself: *made a loop with ribbon.* ***loops, looped, looping***

loud |loud| *adj.* Not quiet: *a loud bang from the cannon.* ***louder, loudest, loudly, loudness***

luck |lŭk| *n.* Good fortune: *will wish you luck in the race.* ***lucky, luckier, luckiest, luckily***

lucky |lŭkʹē| *adj.* Having or bringing good fortune: *a lucky penny.* [see *luck*]

lump |lŭmp| *n.* **1.** A shapeless mass: *a lump of dough.* **2.** A bump or swelling: *a lump on my hand.* ***lumps, lumped, lumping, lumpy, lumpiness***

lung |lŭng| *adj.* Of the lung: *lung operation.* *n.* One of the two organs for breathing air: *left lung.* ***lungs***

lying |līʹĭng| *v.* Telling an untruth: *lying about the accident.* *adj.* Not telling the truth: *the lying thief.* [see *lie*]

M

mad |măd| *adj.* **1.** Very excited; foolish: *mad actions.* **2.** Angry: *mad for not winning.* ***madder, maddest, madden, maddens, maddened, maddening, madly, madness***

madder |mădʹər| *adj.* Angrier: *madder than yesterday.* [see *mad*]

madly |mădʹlē| *adv.* With great energy or power: *is working madly.* [see *mad*]

magic |măjʹĭk| *adj.* Done by using tricks to make things that seem impossible happen: *a magic wand.* ***magical, magically, magician***

mail |māl| *n.* The system by which letters and packages are sent: *delivered by mail.* ***mails, mailed, mailing, mailer***

mailed |māld| *v.* Sent by mail: *mailed the package.* [see *mail*]

make |māk| *v.* To put together: *to make a salad.* ***makes, made, making***

ă **pat** / ā **pay** / â **care** / ä **father** / ĕ **pet** / ē **be** / ĭ **pit** / ī **pie** / î **fierce** / ŏ **pot** / ō **go** / ô **paw, for** / oi **oil** / o͝o **book** / o͞o **boot** / ou **out** / ŭ **cut** / û **fur** / *th* **the** / th **thin** / hw **which** / zh **vision** / ə **ago, item, pencil, atom, circus**

making |mā′kĭng| *v.* Putting together: *making new clothes.* [see *make*]

map |măp| *v.* To make a map, or chart, that shows where things are located: *will map the city streets.* ***maps, mapped, mapping***

mapping |măp′ĭng| *v.* To make a map of: *was mapping the stars in the sky.* [see *map*]

marble |mär′bəl| *adj.* Made of marble: *a marble tabletop. n.* A hard, polished round stone or glass: *a brightly colored marble.* ***marbles, marbled, marbling***

March |märch| *n.* The third month in the year: *a birthday in March.* ***Mar.***

mark |märk| *n.* A spot made on one object by another: *left a mark on the floor. v.* To show clearly: *will mark my place with this paper.* ***marks, marked, marking, marker***

marker |mär′kər| *n.* **1.** Something used to draw or write: *paper and a blue marker.* **2.** A piece of paper, cloth, leather, etc., used to hold, or mark, one's place in a book: *found the marker on page 280.* [see *mark*]

mask |măsk| *n.* A covering that hides or protects the face: *a frightful mask.* ***masks, masked, masking***

matter |măt′ər| *v.* To be important: *won't matter if we lose.* ***matters, mattered***

May |mā| *n.* The fifth month in the year: *the first day of May.*

meal |mēl| *n.* Food served and eaten at one time: *a meal of meat and potatoes.* ***meals***

mean |mēn| *v.* To intend; have as a purpose: *to mean something by her comment.* ***means, meant, meaning, meaner, meanest, meaningful***

means |mēnz| *v.* Intends; has as a purpose: *means to do well.* [see *mean*]

meet |mēt| *v.* To come together by appointment: *to meet at four o'clock.* ***meets, met, meeting***

meeting |mē′tĭng| *n.* A coming together: *a business meeting.* [see *meet*]

melt |mĕlt| *v.* To turn into a liquid by heating: *to melt wax.* ***melts, melted, melting***

middle |mĭd′l| *n.* The point equally distant between two sides or times; center: *middle of the room.*

might |mīt| *n.* Great power, strength, or skill: *the might of the storm.* ***mighty, mightier, mightiest***

mighty |mī′tē| *adj.* Powerful, strong, or skillful: *a mighty lion.* [see *might*]

mild |mīld| *adj.* Not very hot or cold: *a mild winter.* ***milder, mildest, mildly, mildness***

mile |mīl| *n.* A measure of distance equal to 5,280 feet: *drove for one mile.* ***miles, mileage***

mint |mĭnt| *n.* A plant used for flavoring: *lemonade with mint.* ***mints, minted, minting, minty***

mist |mĭst| *n.* Very fine drops of water in the air: *mist on the windshield.* ***mists, misted, misting, misty***

mix |mĭks| *v.* To combine together by stirring: *to mix flour, water, and eggs.* ***mixes, mixed, mixing, mixer, mixture***

Monday |mŭn′dā| *n.* The second day of the week: *starts school on Monday.* ***Mon.***

monster |mŏn′stər| *n.* An imaginary creature that is very large and frightening: *saw an ugly monster.* ***monsters, monstrous, monstrosity***

month |mŭnth| *n.* One of twelve periods of time in a year: *the month of January.* ***months, monthly***

mostly |mōst′lē| *adv.* Mainly; for the most part: *mostly cloudy.* [see *much*]

mouse |mous| *n.* A small furry animal with a long tail: *a gray mouse.* ***mice, mousy***

much |mŭch| *adv.* Greatly: *not much pleased with the painting.* ***more, most, mostly***

music |myōō′zĭk| *n.* An interesting or pleasing combination of sounds: *loud music.* ***musical, musically, musician***

N

nail |nāl| *n.* A thin, pointed piece of metal used to hold things together: *will hammer the nail.* ***nails, nailed, nailing***

nails |nālz| *n.* More than one nail: *tools and nails.* [see *nail*]

near |nîr| *adj.* Close by in space or time: *in the near future.* ***nears, neared, nearing, nearer, nearest, nearness, nearly***

nearest |nîr′ĭst| *adj.* Closest: *the nearest exit.* [see *near*]

nineteen |nīn′tēn′| *adj.* Nine more than ten: *nineteen people. n.* Nine more than ten: *a group of nineteen.* ***nineteens, nineteenth***

nobody |nō′bŏd′ē| *pron.* No person: *nobody allowed inside.*

noise |noiz| *n.* A loud and unpleasant sound: *too much noise.* ***noises, noisy, noisier, noisiest, noisily, noisiness***

none |nŭn| *pron.* Not any: *have none left.*

notebook |nōt′bŏŏks′| *n.* A book with blank pages on which to write: *wrote a poem in my notebook.* ***notebooks***

notebooks |nōt′bŏŏks′| *n.* More than one notebook: *bought two notebooks for school.* [see *notebook*]

November |nō vĕm′bər| *n.* The eleventh month in the year: *took a vacation in November.* ***Nov.***

number |nŭm′bər| *n.* **1.** A numeral connected with a person or thing: *telephone number.* **2.** A numeral: *the next number.* ***numbers, numbered, numbering***

nurse |nûrs| *n.* A person trained to take care of people who are sick: *the doctor and the nurse.* ***nurses, nursed, nursing, nursery***

O

oak |ōk| *adj.* Made of wood from an oak tree: *an oak floor. n.* **1.** A tree with strong wood and acorns: *the oak in the yard.* **2.** The wood from an oak tree: *a chair of oak.* ***oaks***

ocean |ō′shən| *n.* One of the large bodies of salt water that covers almost all of the earth's surface: *swam in the ocean.* ***oceans***

o'clock |ə klŏk′| *adv.* According to the clock: *begins at two o'clock.*

October |ŏk tō′bər| *adj.* Of October: *an October holiday. n.* The tenth month in the year: *a day in October.* ***Oct.***

oil |oil| *n.* A greasy substance that does not mix with water: *a can of oil.* ***oils, oiled, oiling, oily***

old |ōld| *adj.* Not young: *an old tree.* ***older, oldest***

ă **pat** / ā **pay** / â **care** / ä **father** / ĕ **pet** / ē **be** / ĭ **pit** / ī **pie** / î **fierce** / ŏ **pot** / ō **go** / ô **paw, for** / oi **oil** / ŏŏ **book** / ōō **boot** / ou **out** / ŭ **cut** / û **fur** / *th* **the** / th **thin** / hw **which** / zh **vision** / ə **ago, item, pencil, atom, circus**

oldest |ōl′dĭst| *adj.* Having lived for the longest time: *oldest brother.* [see *old*]

omit |ō mĭt′| *v.* To leave out: *to omit the salt.* ***omits, omitted, omitting***

only |ōn′lē| *adj.* By itself; one and no more: *the only window.*

open |ō′pən| *v.* To make or become not shut: *to open the door.* ***opens, opened, opening, openings, openly, opener***

opening |ō′pə nĭng| *n.* A hole: *covered the opening.* [see *open*]

orange |ôr′ĭnj| *n.* A reddish-yellow citrus fruit: *ate an orange.* ***oranges***

ounce |ouns| *n.* A measure of weight equal to one sixteenth of a pound: *one ounce of cheese.* ***ounces, oz.***

outfit |out′fĭt′| *n.* All the articles or clothing necessary for a special purpose: *a skiing outfit.* ***outfits, outfitted, outfitting, outfitter***

outfits |out′fĭts′| *n.* More than one outfit: *outfits for hiking.* [see *outfit*]

own |ōn| *v.* To have: *does own a bicycle.* ***owns, owned, owning, owner, owners***

owner |ō′nər| *n.* A person who owns: *owner of the lost cat.* [see *own*]

P

pack |păk| *v.* To fill with items: *to pack a suitcase.* ***packs, packed, packing, packer***

package |păk′ĭj| *n.* A group of items packed or wrapped together: *mailed a package.* ***packages, packaged, packaging***

packed |păkt| *v.* Filled with items: *packed the box.* [see *pack*]

paddle |păd′l| *v.* To move a boat with a short oar: *to paddle across the lake.* *n.* A piece of wood with a handle at one end, used for mixing, stirring, etc.: *a paddle for stirring cement.* ***paddles, paddled, paddling, paddler***

pain |pān| *n.* A feeling of hurt caused by an injury or sickness: *felt a sudden and sharp pain.* ***pains, painful, painfully, painfulness, painless, painlessly, painlessness***

part |pärt| *n.* Not all: *part of the problem.* ***parts, parted, parting, partner, partly***

partly |pärt′lē| *adv.* In part; in some measure or degree: *partly to blame.* [see *part*]

party |pär′tē| *n.* A group of people gathered together to have fun: *played games at the party.* ***parties, partied, partying***

paste |pāst| *n.* A thick mixture used to stick things together: *has used paste to put photos in the album.* ***pastes, pasted, pasting, pasty***

peek |pēk| *v.* To look at secretly: *to peek into the room.* ***peeks, peeked, peeking***

phone |fōn| *n.* An instrument for sending and receiving speech over long distances; a telephone: *talked on the phone.* ***phones, phoned, phoning***

picnic |pĭk′nĭk| *adj.* Of or for a picnic: *picnic lunch.* *n.* A meal that is eaten outside: *made salad for the picnic.* ***picnics, picnicked, picnicking, picnicker***

picture |pĭk′chər| *n.* A drawing, painting, or photograph of someone or something: *a picture of my family.* ***pictures, pictured, picturing***

pile |pīl| *n.* A large amount of things stacked on top of each other: *a pile of clothes.* ***piles, piled, piling***

pillow |pĭl′ō| *n.* A stuffed cloth case that is used to support a person's head while lying down: *a pillow on the bed.* ***pillows***

plane |plān| *n.* A machine with propellers or jet engines that make it fly; an airplane: *landed the plane.* ***planes***

playmate |plā′māt′| *n.* A person who plays with someone else: *playmate in the neighborhood.* ***playmates***

plenty |plĕn′tē| *n.* A full supply of all that is needed: *plenty of water.* ***plentiful, plentifully***

plum |plŭm| *n.* A juicy purple fruit with a smooth skin and a pit: *a plum and a pear.* ***plums***

pocket |pŏk′ĭt| *n.* A small bag for holding things, sewn into clothing: *keys in her pocket.* ***pockets, pocketed, pocketing, pocketful***

poem |pō′əm| *n.* A form of writing with words arranged in verses that often rhyme: *a poem about summer.* ***poems, poet, poetry***

point |point| *n.* The main purpose or idea: *understood the point you made.* ***points, pointed, pointing, pointless, pointer***

pool |pool| *n.* A tank of water for swimming: *swam to the edge of the pool.* ***pools***

porch |pôrch| *n.* A covered area built onto a house: *on the front porch.* ***porches***

post |pōst| *n.* A straight piece of wood or metal used to hold something up: *nailed to the post.* ***posts, posted, posting***

poster |pō′stər| *n.* A large printed notice put out for the public to see: *a circus poster.* ***posters***

pound |pound| *n.* A unit of weight equal to sixteen ounces: *one pound of fish.* ***pounds, pounded, pounding, lb.***

pour |pôr| *v.* To flow or cause to flow steadily: *to pour milk.* ***pours, poured, pouring***

pouring |pôr′ĭng| *v.* Flowing or causing to flow steadily: *pouring from the hose.* *adj.* Flowing: *pouring rain.* [see *pour*]

power |pou′ər| *adj.* Run by a motor: *a power drill.* *n.* Strength: *the power of five people.* ***powers, powered, powering, powerful, powerfully***

press |prĕs| *n.* A machine for printing books, magazines, and newspapers: *operated the press.* *v.* To put force on something: *to press the door shut.* ***presses, pressed, pressing***

pretend |prĭ tĕnd′| *v.* To make believe: *to pretend you are flying.* ***pretends, pretended, pretending, pretender***

price |prīs| *n.* The cost or amount of money for which something is bought or sold: *for the same price.* ***prices, priced, pricing***

prices |prī′sĭz| *n.* Costs; *low prices for gas.* [see *price*]

pride |prīd| *n.* Pleasure in one's actions or worth; self-respect: *takes pride in her schoolwork.* ***prides, prided, priding, prideful***

print |prĭnt| *n.* Letters in ink, stamped by type: *easy-to-read print.* *v.* To write in block letters, like those seen in print: *will print my name.* ***prints, printed, printing, printer***

prize |prīz| *n.* An award won in a contest or game: *tried to win the prize.* ***prizes, prized, prizing***

ă pat / ā pay / â care / ä father / ĕ pet / ē be / ĭ pit / ī pie / î fierce / ŏ pot / ō go / ô paw, for / oi oil / ŏŏ book / ōō boot / ou out / ŭ cut / û fur / *th* the / th thin / hw which / zh vision / ə ago, item, pencil, atom, circus

proud |proud| *adj.* Feeling very pleased or satisfied: *a proud winner.* ***prouder, proudest, proudly***

provide |prə **vīd**′| *v.* **1.** To prepare ahead of time: *to provide lunch and dinner.* **2.** To give what is needed: *will provide pens and paper.* ***provides, provided, providing, provider***

purse |pûrs| *n.* A handbag or pocketbook: *a leather purse.* ***purses***

Q

queen |kwēn| *n.* A female monarch, or ruler; a king's wife: *the queen on her throne.* ***queens, queenly***

quiet |**kwī**′ĭt| *adj.* Peaceful; with little noise: *a quiet time.* ***quieter, quietest, quietly, quiteness***

quit |kwĭt| *v.* **1.** To give up: *to quit the team.* **2.** To stop: *will quit painting my room before noon.* ***quits, quitted, quitting, quitter***

quite |kwīt| *adv.* Completely: *quite clear.*

R

race |rās| *n.* A contest to find the fastest: *an automobile race.* ***races, raced, racing, racer***

races |**rā**′sĭz| *n.* More than one race: *bicycle races.* [see *race*]

rack |răk| *n.* A bar or stand on which to hang things: *a metal rack for clothes.* ***racks***

rain |rān| *v.* To fall in drops of water from clouds: *to rain heavily.* ***rains, rained, raining, rainy, rainier, rainiest***

rainy |**rā**′nē| *adj.* Having rain: *a rainy afternoon.*—**Rainy day**—A time of need in the future. [see *rain*]

ranch |rănch| *n.* A large farm for raising animals: *herds of cattle at the ranch.*—**Ranch house**—A one-story house. ***ranches, rancher***

range |rānj| *v.* To travel, wander, or roam over a wide area: *will range from place to place.* ***ranges, ranged, ranging, ranger, rangers***

ranger |**rān**′jər| *n.* A person who guards a forest or park: *the park ranger.* [see *range*]

ray |rā| *n.* A narrow beam of light: *a bright ray.* ***rays***

read |rēd| *v.* To look at something written and understand the meaning: *to read the headlines and the editorials in the newspaper.* ***reads, reading, reader, readers***

reader |**rē**′dər| *n.* A person who reads: *a reader of poetry, plays, and short stories.* [see *read*]

real |**rē**′əl| *adj.* **1.** True; not made up: *the real story.* **2.** Not imitation or fake: *real flowers.* ***really, realize, realist, realistic***

recover |rĭ **kŭv**′ər| *v.* To get back something lost or stolen: *to recover the missing wallet.* ***recovers, recovered, recovering, recovery***

remind |rĭ **mīnd**′| *v.* To make a person remember something: *to remind him of the meeting.* ***reminds, reminded, reminding, reminder***

repair |rĭ **pâr**′| *v.* To mend or fix: *to repair the damage.* ***repairs, repaired, repairing, repairer***

replace |rĭ **plās**′| *v.* To fill or take the place of: *will replace the exact number of eggs I use.* ***replaces, replaced, replacing, replacement***

return |rĭ tûrn′| *v.* To bring, send, put, or give back: *to return the lost wallet.* ***returns, returned, returning, returnable***

returning |rĭ tûr′nĭng| *v.* Bringing, sending, putting, or giving back: *was returning what I borrowed.* [see *return*]

reward |rĭ wôrd′| *n.* **1.** Money given or offered for the return of something lost, the capture of a criminal, information, etc.: *received a ten-dollar reward for finding the lost kitten.* **2.** Something given or received in return for doing something; a prize: *got a reward for rescuing the child.* ***rewards, rewarded, rewarding***

rich |rĭch| *adj.* Having a lot of money or wealth: *a rich uncle.* ***richer, richest, richly, riches***

ripe |rīp| *adj.* Completely grown and ready for eating: *ripe fruit.* ***riper, ripest, ripen, ripens, ripened, ripening, ripeness***

river |rĭv′ər| *n.* A natural stream of water that flows into another body of water: *floating down to the river.* ***rivers***

roar |rôr| *n.* A loud, deep sound: *the animal's roar.* ***roars, roared, roaring, roarer***

roll |rōl| *v.* To turn over and over: *to roll the ball across the floor.* ***rolls, rolled, rolling, roller***

rolled |rōld| *v.* Turned over and over: *rolled down the stairs.* [see *roll*]

root |ro͞ot| *n.* The part of a plant that grows underground: *dug down the root.* ***roots, rooted, rooting***

rule |ro͞ol| *n.* A statement of what should and should not be done: *one rule of the game.* ***rules, ruled, ruling, ruler***

rules |ro͞olz| *n.* More than one rule: *followed the rules.* [see *rule*]

S

sack |săk| *n.* A large bag made of rough cloth: *stuffed dirty clothes into a sack.* ***sacks***

saddle |săd′l| *n.* A seat for riding on the back of a horse or similar animal: *a leather saddle.* ***saddles, saddled, saddling, saddler***

sail |sāl| *n.* A piece of material that catches the wind to make a boat move: *raised the sail much higher.* ***sails, sailed, sailing, sailor***

sank |săngk| *v.* Went under the surface of or to the bottom of some liquid: *sank in the pond.* [see *sink*]

Saturday |săt′ər dā′| *n.* The seventh day of the week: *soccer practice on Saturday.* **Sat.**

save |sāv| *v.* **1.** To set aside or store up for future use: *to save money.* **2.** To rescue or protect from danger: *to save him from the fire.* ***saves, saved, saving, savings, saver***

saves |sāvz| *v.* **1.** Sets aside or stores up for future use: *saves all kinds of buttons.* **2.** Rescues or protects from danger: *saves people from burning buildings.* [see *save*]

scale |skāl| *n.* **1.** A series of musical tones: *played a scale on the piano.* **2.** One of the thin, hard parts that covers the outside of fish and reptiles: *a scale from the fish.* ***scales, scaled, scaling, scaly***

scold |skōld| *v.* To blame angrily: *to scold for arriving late.* ***scolds, scolded, scolding***

ă pat / ā pay / â care / ä father / ĕ pet / ē be / ĭ pit / ī pie / î fierce / ŏ pot / ō go / ô paw, for / oi oil / o͝o book / o͞o boot / ou out / ŭ cut / û fur / *th* the / th thin / hw which / zh vision / ə ago, item, pencil, atom, circus

score |skôr| *n.* The total points made in a game, test, or contest: *a score of 90.* ***scores, scored, scoring, scorer***

scrap |skrăp| *n.* A small piece: *a scrap of paper.* ***scraps***

scrape |skrāp| *v.* To smooth or clean by rubbing: *to scrape your boots.* *n.* A scratched or scraped place: *a scrape on my knee.* ***scrapes, scraped, scraping, scraper***

scream |skrēm| *n.* A loud, sharp cry or sound: *heard a scream.* ***screams, screamed, screaming, screamer***

scrub |skrŭb| *v.* To wash by rubbing: *to scrub your face.* ***scrubs, scrubbed, scrubbing, scrubber***

season |sē′zən| *n.* One of the four parts in a year; spring, summer, fall, or winter: *a snowy season.* ***seasons, seasoned, seasoning, seasonal***

seat |sēt| *n.* A place to sit: *an empty seat.* ***seats, seated, seating***

second |sĕk′ənd| *n.* One of sixty periods of time in a minute: *lasts only one second.* *adj.* After the first: *second door on the left.* ***seconds, seconded, seconding, secondly***

seem |sēm| *v.* To appear to be be: *to seem happy.* ***seems, seemed, seeming***

seemed |sēmd| *v.* Appeared to be: *seemed pleased.* [see *seem*]

sense |sĕns| *n.* Good judgment; intelligence: *didn't use very much sense.* ***senses, sensed, sensing, senseless***

September |sĕp **tĕm′**bər| *n.* The ninth month in the year: *the beginning of September.* ***Sept.***

seven |**sĕv′**ən| *adj.* One more than six: *seven cats.* ***sevens, seventh, sevenths***

seventh |**sĕv′**ənth| *adj.* Next after the sixth: *the seventh grade.* [see *seven*]

shake |shāk| *v.* **1.** To move quickly from side to side or up and down: *to shake in the wind.* **2.** To grasp hands in greeting another person: *to shake firmly.* ***shakes, shook, shaking, shaky, shakier, shakiest, shakily, shaker***

shame |shām| *n.* A fact to be sorry about: *a shame to miss the party.* ***shames, shamed, shaming, shameless, shamelessness, shameful***

shape |shāp| *n.* A form: *the shape of a ball.* ***shapes, shaped, shaping, shapeless, shapely***

share |shâr| *n.* **1.** A part given or belonging to one person: *an equal share.* *v.* To divide and give away in parts: *to share an orange.* **2.** To use with others: *will share the same room.* ***shares, shared, sharing, sharer***

sharing |**shâr′**ĭng| *v.* Using with others: *sharing our books.* [see *share*]

shed |shĕd| *n.* A small building used for storage: *tools in the shed.* ***sheds, shedding***

sheep |shēp| *n.* An animal with thick wool and hooves: *sheep in the meadow.* ***sheepish***

sheet |shēt| *n.* A large piece of cloth used to cover a bed: *slept under the sheet.* ***sheets***

shell |shĕl| *n.* The hard outer covering of some animals: *The turtle's shell.* ***shells, shelled, shelling***

she's |shēz| Contraction for *she is: since she's late.*

shine |shīn| *n.* Brightness: *the shine from the flashlight.* *v.* To make bright; polish: *to shine with a clean cloth.* ***shines, shined, shone, shining, shiny, shinier, shiniest***

shining |shī′nĭng| *v.* Making bright; polishing: *is shining shoes. adj.* Bright: *shining star.* [see *shine*]

shirt |shûrt| *n.* A piece of clothing worn on the upper part of the body: *buttoned my shirt.* ***shirts***

shock |shŏk| *n.* **1.** A sudden feeling caused by electricity passing through the body: *a shock from the loose wire.* **2.** A sudden, upsetting happening: *was a shock to me.* ***shocks, shocked, shocking, shockingly***

shore |shôr| *n.* The land along the edge of an ocean, river, or lake: *shells on the shore.* ***shores***

shout |shout| *n.* A loud call or cry: *a shout of joy when the parade began.* ***shouts, shouted, shouting***

show |shō| *v.* To put in sight; let be seen: *to show her stamp collection.* ***shows, showed, shown, showing***

shower |shou′ər| *n.* **1.** A bath in which water sprays down on a person: *used soap in the shower.* **2.** A brief fall of rain: *an afternoon shower.* ***showers, showered, showering***

shown |shōn| *v.* Put in sight; let be seen: *had shown me his new navy-blue coat.* [see *show*]

sidewalk |sīd′wôk′| *n.* A place by the edge of a street where people can walk: *stepped over every big crack in the sidewalk.* ***sidewalks***

sideways |sīd′wāz| *adv.* With one side facing forward: *stepped sideways through the crowd.*

silk |sĭlk| *n.* A soft, shiny material: *a jacket lined with silk. adj.* Made of silk: *a silk tie.* ***silks, silky, silkier, silkiest, silken***

silver |sĭl′vər| *n.* A soft, shiny white metal: *made of silver. adj.* Shiny gray: *a silver crayon.* ***silvers, silvered, silvery***

since |sĭns| *prep.* From a past time until now: *since last month.*

single |sĭng′gəl| *adj.* Only one: *a single sheet of paper.* **—Single file—**A line of people or things arranged one behind the other. ***singles, singly, singular***

sink |sĭngk| *v.* To go under the surface of or to the bottom of some liquid: *will sink in the ocean. n.* A shallow tub used for washing: *a sink filled with water.* ***sinks, sank, sunk, sunken, sinking***

sir |sûr| *n.* A title used instead of a man's name: *sir or madam.* ***sirs***

sit |sĭt| *v.* To rest with the back upright and the weight off the feet: *to sit in a chair.* ***sits, sat, sitting, sitter***

sitting |sĭt′ĭng| *v.* Resting upright: *sitting on a bench.* [see *sit*]

six |sĭks| *adj.* One more than five: *six apples.* ***sixes, sixth, sixths***

sixteen |sĭks′tēn′| *adj.* Six more than ten: *sixteen years old. n.* Six more than ten: *a group of sixteen.* ***sixteens, sixteenth***

sixth |sĭksth| *adj.* Next after the fifth: *the sixth person. n.* The next after the fifth: *the sixth in line.* [see *six*]

size |sīz| *n.* **1.** The height, length, and width of something: *the size of our house.* **2.** A series of measurements used for things made, such as clothes: *took a smaller size.* ***sizes, sized, sizing***

ă **pat** / ā **pay** / â **care** / ä **father** / ĕ **pet** / ē **be** / ĭ **pit** / ī **pie** / î **fierce** / ŏ **pot** / ō **go** / ô **paw**, **for** / oi **oil** / ŏŏ **book** / ōō **boot** / ou **out** / ŭ **cut** / û **fur** / *th* **the** / th **thin** / hw **which** / zh **vision** / ə **ago**, **item**, **pencil**, **atom**, **circus**

skate |skāt| *n.* A special shoe that has metal blade or small wheels for gliding over smooth surfaces: *laced my skate. v.* To move on skates: *to skate in a circle.* ***skates, skated, skating, skater***

skating |**skā**´tĭng| *adj.* Of skating: *skating skirt. v.* Moving on skates: *was skating with friends.* [see *skate*]

skill |skĭl| *n.* The ability to do something well through training and practice: *has skill in spelling.* ***skills, skilled, skillful, skillfully, skillfullness***

sleep |slēp| *v.* To rest the body and mind: *to sleep at night.* ***sleeps, slept, sleeping, sleepy, sleepier, sleepiest, sleepily, sleeper***

sleepy |**slē**´pē| *adj.* Needing or ready for sleep: *sleepy child.* [see *sleep*]

slept |slĕpt| *v.* Rested the body and mind: *slept for eight hours.* [see *sleep*]

slice |slīs| *v.* To cut into thin, flat pieces: *to slice meat.* ***slices, sliced, slicing, slicer***

sliced |slīst| *adj.* In thin, flat pieces: *ate sliced cheese. v.* Cut into thin, flat pieces: *sliced a loaf of bread.* [see *slice*]

slid |slĭd| *v.* Moved easily: *slid into third base.* [see *slide*]

slide |slīd| *n.* A smooth surface for moving easily on: *a metal slide in the playground. v.* To move easily: *to slide down the hill.* ***slides, slid, sliding, slider***

sliding |**slī**´dĭng| *adj.* Moving easily: *sliding window. v.* Moving easily: *was sliding on skis.* [see *slide*]

slip |slĭp| *v.* To slide suddenly without control: *to slip on the ice.* ***slips, slipped, slipping, slippery, slipper, slippers, slipperiness***

slow |slō| *adj.* Not moving quickly: *a slow train on the track.* ***slows, slower, slowest, slowed, slowing, slowly, slowness***

slowly |**slō**´lē| *adv.* Not quickly: *drove slowly.* [see *slow*]

smile |smīl| *v.* To show happiness or amusement: *to smile with delight. n.* An expression on the face showing that a person is happy or amused: *a big smile from every student.* ***smiles, smiled, smiling, smiler***

smoke |smōk| *n.* A cloud of gas given off by something burning: *smoke from the fire.* ***smokes, smoked, smoking, smoker, smoky, smokier, smokiest***

snap |snăp| *v.* To break with a sudden, sharp sound: *will snap the small twig in half.* ***snaps, snapped, snapping, snapper***

sneaker |**snē**´kər| *n.* A canvas shoe with a rubber sole: *found the matching sneaker.* ***sneakers***

sneakers |**snē**´kərz| *n.* More than one sneaker: *white sneakers for tennis.* [see *sneaker*]

sob |sŏb| *n.* The act or sound of crying with gasps of breath: *heard the child's sob. v.* To cry with gasps of breath: *will sob when sad.* ***sobs, sobbed, sobbing***

soil |soil| *n.* Dirt: *growing in soil.* ***soils, soiled, soiling***

sore |sôr| *adj.* Painful; tender: *soothed my sore toe.* ***sores, sorely, sorer, sorest, soreness***

sort |sôrt| *n.* A kind; type: *this sort of animal.* ***sorts, sorted, sorting, sorter***

space |spās| *n.* **1.** The region beyond the earth's atmosphere: *a rocket in space.* **2.** A limited place or area: *little space in the tent.* ***spaces, spaced, spacing, spacer***

speak |spēk| *v.* To say words: *to speak very softly.* ***speaks, spoke, spoken, speaking, speaker***

spend |spĕnd| *v.* **1.** To pay out: *will spend five dollars.* **2.** To use up: *to spend more energy.* ***spends, spent, spending, spender***

spin |spĭn| *v.* To turn around quickly: *to spin until dizzy. n.* A quick turn: *one more spin.* ***spins, spun, spinning, spinner***

spoke |spōk| *v.* Said words: *spoke to the teacher.* [see *speak*]

sport |spôrt| *n.* A game in which a person exercises: *the sport of basketball.* ***sports, sporting***

stable |**stā**′bəl| *n.* A building where horses and cattle are kept: *hay in the stable.* ***stables, stabled***

stake |stāk| *n.* A stick driven into the ground for holding or marking something: *a stake for the badminton net.* ***stakes, staked, staking***

steal |stēl| *v.* To take something that belongs to someone else: *since robbers steal valuables.* ***steals, stole, stolen, stealing***

steam |stēm| *n.* Hot water in the form of gas or mist: *steam from the boiling kettle.* ***steams, steamed, steaming, steamy, steamer***

steel |stēl| *adj.* Made of steel: *a steel bridge. n.* A hard and strong metal: *tools made from steel.* ***steels, steely***

steep |stēp| *adj.* Having an almost straight up-and-down slope: *climbed a steep hill.* ***steeper, steepest***

stocking |**stŏk**′ĭng| *n.* A knitted covering for the leg and foot: *wore a silk stocking.* **—In one's stocking feet—**Wearing stockings without shoes. ***stocking***

stole |stōl| *v.* Took something dishonestly: *stole money.* [see *steal*]

stories |**stôr**′ēz| *n.* More than one story: *stories about history.* [see *story*]

story |**stôr**′ē| *n.* A tale about something that has happened, either true or made up: *a funny story.* ***stories***

strange |strānj| *adj.* Unusual; odd: *a strange noise.* ***stranger, strangest, strangely, strangeness***

straw |strô| *n.* Dry stalks of grain: *straw for the horses.* ***straws***

stream |strēm| *n.* A small body of flowing water: *fished in the stream for large trout.* ***streams, streamed, streaming, streamer***

strike |strīk| *v.* **1.** To stop work for better pay, shorter hours, etc.: *workers who will strike next week.* **2.** To hit: *will strike it with your fist.* **—Strike out—**In baseball, to pitch three strikes to a batter, putting the batter out. ***strikes, struck, striking, striker***

strong |strông| *adj.* Having a great amount of strength or power: *a strong bear.* ***stronger, strongest, strongly***

ă pat / ā pay / â care / ä father / ĕ pet / ē be / ĭ pit / ī pie / î fierce / ŏ pot / ō go / ô paw, for / oi oil / o͝o book / o͞o boot / ou out / ŭ cut / û fur / *th* the / th thin / hw which / zh vision / ə ago, item, pencil, atom, circus

study |stŭd′ē| *v.* To try to learn: *to study science.* ***studies, studied, studying, studious, student***

sum |sŭm| *n.* **1.** An amount of money: *a sum of five dollars.* **2.** The number gotten from adding two or more numbers together: *to find the sum of 2 plus 6 plus 13.* ***sums, summed, summing, summary***

Sunday |sŭn′dā| *adj.* Of Sunday: *Sunday dinner. n.* The first day of the week: *a picnic on Sunday.* ***Sun.***

sure |shoo̅r| *adj.* Certain: *is sure it will rain.* ***surer, surest, surely***

sweep |swēp| *v.* To clear or take away: *to sweep the dust.* ***sweeps, swept, sweeping, sweeper***

swift |swĭft| *adj.* Moving very fast: *a swift swimmer in the race.* ***swifter, swiftest, swiftly***

swim |swĭm| *v.* To move in water by using arms, legs, or fins: *will swim in the lake.* ***swims, swam, swum, swimming, swimmer***

swing |swĭng| *n.* A seat hung from ropes in which a person can sit and move back and forth: *the swing at the park.* ***swings, swung, swinging, swinger***

sword |sôrd| *n.* A weapon with a long sharp blade attached to a handle: *the knight's sword.* ***swords***

T

team |tēm| *n.* A group of people playing or working together: *a hockey team.* ***teams, teamed, teaming***

tear |tîr| *n.* A drop of liquid coming from the eye: *wiped away a tear.* ***tears, teared, tearing, tearful***

tear |târ| *v.* To make a hole by ripping: *to tear a sleeve.* ***tears, tore, torn, tearing***

teeth |tēth| *n.* More than one tooth: *white teeth.* [see *tooth*]

tend |tĕnd| *v.* To be likely: *to tend to sleep late.* ***tends, tended, tending, tender***

thick |thĭk| *adj.* Having much space between two sides: *thick doors and walls.* — **Through thick and thin**—In both good and bad times. ***thicker, thickest, thickly, thickness***

thousand |thou′zənd| *adj.* Ten times one hundred: *earned a thousand dollars.* ***thousands, thousandth***

thread |thrĕd| *n.* Thin strands, or lengths, of spun and twisted cotton, silk, nylon, etc., used for sewing: *blue thread for sewing the shirt.* ***threads, threaded, threading, threader***

throw |thrō| *n.* A toss: *a throw to the catcher. v.* To send through the air; toss: *will throw the ball.* ***throws, threw, thrown, throwing, thrower***

ticket |tĭk′ĭt| *n.* **1.** A card or paper that gives certain rights to the person who holds it: *a ticket to the circus.* **2.** A tag or label attached to something to show a price, tell who owns it, etc.: *a ticket sewn on a shirt.* ***tickets, ticketed, ticketing***

tin |tĭn| *n.* A soft silver-white metal: *a box made of tin.* ***tins, tinned, tinning, tinny***

tiny |tī′nē| *adj.* Very small: *a tiny kitten.* ***tinier, tiniest***

tire |tīr| *v.* To make or become weary: *to tire after running.* ***tires, tired, tiring, tireless, tiresome***

tired |tīrd| *adj.* Weary, or worn out: *too tired to stay awake.* [see *tire*]

ton |tŭn| *n.* A unit of weight equal to 2,000 pounds: *weighed a ton.* ***tons***

tooth |to͞oth| *n.* One of the hard, bony parts in the mouth, used for chewing and biting: *one loose tooth.* ***teeth, toothy***

tore |tôr| *v.* Made a hole by ripping: *tore the cloth.* [see *tear*]

tower |**tou′**ər| *n.* A tall building: *the bell in the tower.* ***towers, towered, towering***

trace |trās| *n.* **1.** A small amount: *a trace of dirt.* **2.** A drawing done by tracing: *a trace of the circle. v.* To copy by drawing over lines seen through thin paper: *to trace a picture.* ***traces, traced, tracing, tracer***

trap |trăp| *n.* A trick used to catch a person by surprise: *a sneaky trap.* ***traps, trapped, trapping, trapper***

tribe |trīb| *n.* A group of people with the same ancestors and traditions: *from the same tribe.* ***tribes, tribal***

trick |trĭk| *n.* A clever or skillful act: *the dog's new trick.* ***tricks, tricked, tricking, tricky, trickier, trickiest, trickster***

trim |trĭm| *v.* To make neat by cutting away unnecessary parts: *to trim the plants.* ***trims, trimmed, trimming, trimmer***

trust |trŭst| *n.* A strong belief in someone's honesty, truthfulness, power, etc.: *has your trust.* ***trusts, trusted, trusting, trustful, trustless, trustiness***

Tuesday |**to͞oz′** dā′| *adj.* Of Tuesday: *a Tuesday meeting. n.* The third day of the week: *will mail by Tuesday.* ***Tues.***

turtle |**tûr′**tl| *n.* A reptile whose body is enclosed in a hard round shell: *a turtle in the pond.* ***turtles***

twenty |**twĕn′**tē| *adj.* Two times ten: *twenty minutes ago.* ***twenties, twentieth***

twenty-five |twĕn′tē **fīv′**| *adj.* Five more than twenty: *counted twenty-five times.* ***twenty-fives, twenty-fifth***

U

unlock |ŭn **lŏk′**| *v.* To open the lock of: *hard to unlock.* [see *lock*]

until |ŭn **tĭl′**| *conj.* Up to the time when: *until it freezes. prep.* Up to the time of: *slept until noon.*

W

wade |wād| *v.* To walk slowly and with difficulty through water, mud, or snow: *to wade across the stream. n.* A slow and difficult walk: *a wade into the ocean.* ***wades, waded, wading***

wait |wāt| *v.* To stay in a place until something happens or someone comes: *to wait for the bus.* ***waits, waited, waiting, waiter, waitress***

waiting |**wā′**tĭng| *v.* Staying until something happens or someone comes: *waiting for the rain to stop.* [see *wait*]

ă pat / ā pay / â care / ä father / ĕ pet / ē be / ĭ pit / ī pie / î fierce / ŏ pot / ō go / ô paw, for / oi oil / o͝o book / o͞o boot / ou out / ŭ cut / û fur / *th* the / th thin / hw which / zh vision / ə ago, item, pencil, atom, circus

wake |wāk| *v.* To stop sleeping: *to wake at seven o'clock.* ***wakes, waked, woke, waking, waken, wakens, wakened, wakening***

waste |wāst| *n.* Material to be thrown away; garbage: *threw the waste into a bag.* ***wastes, wasted, wasting, wasteful, wastefully, waster***

weak |wēk| *adj.* Not having power; faint: *a weak sound.* ***weaker, weakest, weakly, weakness***

wear |wâr| *v.* To have on or put on the body: *to wear a coat.* ***wears, wore, worn, wearing***

Wednesday |wĕnz′dā′| *n.* The fourth day of the week: *stayed until Wednesday.* ***Wed.***

weekend |wēk′ĕnd′| *n.* The time between Friday night and Sunday night: *a weekend away from home.* ***weekends***

wheel |wēl| *n.* **1.** Something shaped or used like a wheel: *to steer with the wheel.* **2.** A ring, either solid or with spokes, that turns on its center: *the wheel on the old covered wagon.* ***wheels, wheeled, wheeling***

whip |wĭp| *n.* A flexible strap attached to a handle: *snapped the whip. v.* To beat eggs, batter, etc.: *will whip a dozen eggs.* ***whips, whipped, whipping***

wind |wīnd| *v.* To wrap or fold around something: *to wind yarn into a ball.* ***winds, wound, winding***

wind |wĭnd| *n.* Air that is moving: *knocked down by the wind.* ***windy, windier, windiest, winds***

windy |wĭn′dē| *adj.* Having much wind: *a windy day.* [see *wind*]

woke |wōk| *v.* Stopped sleeping: *woke late in the day.* [see *wake*]

woman |wo͝om′ən| *n.* An adult female human being: *the woman with black hair.* ***women, womanly***

women |wĭm′ĭn| *n.* More than one woman: *talking with the women in our town.* [see *woman*]

won't |wōnt| Contraction for *will not: won't finish on time.*

wore |wôr| *v.* Had on or put on the body: *wore a heavy sweater under my jacket.* [see *wear*]

worn |wôrn| *v.* Had on or put on the body: *the shirt you had worn yesterday. adj.* Damaged because of use or wear: *worn, dirty shirt.* [see *wear*]

worry |wûr′ē| *v.* To feel or cause to feel troubled or uneasy: *to worry them by coming home late.* ***worries, worried, worrying, worrier***

worth |wûrth| *n.* Value, usefulness, or importance: *gems of great worth.* ***worthy, worthless, worthlessness, worthiness***

wound |wound| *adj.* Wrapped or folded around: *wound tightly.* —|wo͞ond| *n.* An injury or hurt: *a knee wound.* [see *wind*]

wrap |răp| *v.* To cover with paper and tie up: *will wrap the gift.* ***wraps, wrapped, wrapping, wrapper***

write |rīt| *v.* **1.** To form words or symbols with a pen, pencil, or other instrument: *to write your name.* **2.** To make up stories, books poems, or articles: *to write for the newspaper.* ***writes, wrote, writing, written, writer, writers***

writer |rī′tər| *n.* A person who writes; an author: *a writer of mysteries.* [see *write*]

wrong |rông| *adj.* Not correct: *gave me the wrong answer.* ***wrongs, wronged, wronging, wrongly***

Y

yard |yärd| *n.* **1.** An area of ground around a house or other building: *played outside in the yard.* **2.** An area used for a certain kind of business: *a coal yard.* ***yards, yardage***

yellow |yĕl′ō| *adj.* Having the color yellow: *a yellow sweater. n.* The color of lemons and gold: *leaves of yellow and red.* ***yellows, yellowed, yellowing***

COVER DESIGN:
Design Five

PHOTOGRAPHY:
Joseph Sachs

TEXT ILLUSTRATIONS:
John Edwards & Associates
pages 17, 43, 55, 79, 95

Tracy Sabin
page 3

All other art by Will Winslow

PROJECT ASSISTANCE:
Chameleon Publishing Services

ă pat / ā pay / â care / ä father / ĕ pet / ē be / ĭ pit / ī pie / î fierce / ŏ pot / ō go / ô paw, for / oi oil / o͝o book / o͞o boot / ou out / ŭ cut / û fur / *th* the / th thin / hw which / zh vision / ə ago, item, pencil, atom, circus